# Statistical Analysis of Understory Vegetation Data from Valley Forge National Historical Park, Pennsylvania, 1993–2003

Technical Report NPS/NER/NRTR—2008/118

Duane R. Diefenbach[1], Wendy C. Vreeland[2], and Kristina M. Heister[3]

[1] U.S. Geological Survey
Pennsylvania Cooperative Fish and Wildlife Research Unit
Pennsylvania State University
University Park, PA 16802

[2] Pennsylvania Cooperative Fish and Wildlife Research Unit
Pennsylvania State University
University Park, PA 16802

[3] National Park Service
Valley Forge National Historical Park
1400 North Outer Line Drive
King of Prussia, PA 19406-1009

April 2008

U.S. Department of the Interior
National Park Service
Northeast Region
Philadelphia, Pennsylvania

The Northeast Region of the National Park Service (NPS) comprises national parks and related areas in 13 New England and Mid-Atlantic states. The diversity of parks and their resources are reflected in their designations as national parks, seashores, historic sites, recreation areas, military parks, monuments and memorials, and rivers and trails. Biological, physical, and social science research results, natural resource inventory and monitoring data, scientific literature reviews, bibliographies, and proceedings of technical workshops and conferences related to these park units are disseminated through the NPS/NER Technical Report (NRTR) and Natural Resources Report (NRR) series. The reports are a continuation of series with previous acronyms of NPS/PHSO, NPS/MAR, NPS/BSO-RNR, and NPS/NERBOST. Individual parks may also disseminate information through their own report series.

Natural Resources Reports are the designated medium for information on technologies and resource management methods; "how to" resource management papers; proceedings of resource management workshops or conferences; and natural resource program descriptions and resource action plans.

Technical Reports are the designated medium for initially disseminating data and results of biological, physical, and social science research that addresses natural resource management issues; natural resource inventories and monitoring activities; scientific literature reviews; bibliographies; and peer-reviewed proceedings of technical workshops, conferences, or symposia.

Mention of trade names or commercial products does not constitute endorsement or recommendation for use by the National Park Service.

This report was accomplished under Cooperative Agreement H4560030064, Task Agreement No. 023 with assistance from the NPS. The statements, findings, conclusions, recommendations, and data in this report are solely those of the author(s), and do not necessarily reflect the views of the U.S. Department of the Interior, National Park Service.

Print copies of reports in these series, produced in limited quantity and only available as long as the supply lasts, or preferably, file copies on CD, may be obtained by sending a request to the address on the back cover. Print copies also may be requested from the NPS Technical Information Center (TIC), Denver Service Center, PO Box 25287, Denver, CO 80225-0287. A copy charge may be involved. To order from TIC, refer to document D-107.

This report may also be available as a downloadable portable document format file from the Internet at http://www.nps.gov/nero/science/.

Please cite this publication as:

Diefenbach, D., W. Vreeland, and K. M. Heister. 2008. Statistical Analysis of Understory Vegetation Data from Valley Forge National Historical Park, Pennsylvania, 1993–2003. Technical Report NPS/NER/NRTR— 2008/118. National Park Service. Philadelphia, PA.

NPS D-107   April 2008

# Table of Contents

Tables

Tables (continued)

Figures

# Appendixes

# Executive Summary

A fixed-plot monitoring system was implemented in 1992 to evaluate vegetative communities in two large wooded areas at Valley Forge National Historical Park. The objectives of this monitoring system are to: 1) describe the existing understory plant community on Mount Misery and Mount Joy in terms of species richness and abundance; and 2) determine changes in abundance and species composition of understory plant communities in fenced and unfenced plots over time. This report summarizes the data collected in these plots in 1993, 1995–1996, 1998, and 2003, and presents the results of statistical analyses of the data to determine if specific vegetative changes have occurred over time.

Thirty vegetation sample sites were randomly located on Mount Misery and Mount Joy (15 in each area). At each sample site, paired plots were established where one plot was fenced to exclude deer but no other herbivores. The unfenced control plots were located 36.5 m (119.75 ft) from the center of the fenced plots in a random direction (except three plots were located 20–27.4 m [65.6–90 ft] away). Each plot was 2×2 m (6.5×6.5 ft) in size. Most tree, shrub, vine, and herbaceous vegetation was identified to species, although some vegetation was identified only to genera. The number of tree seedlings was enumerated in all plots.

Species richness was greater on Mount Joy than on Mount Misery for each of the years, and in both areas generally increased over time in fenced plots and exhibited a slight decline over time in unfenced plots. Between 1993 and 2003 on Mount Misery, the total number of species increased from 31 to 41 species in fenced plots, and decreased from 27 to 23 species in unfenced plots. On Mount Joy, the total number of species increased from 56 to 71 species in fenced plots and declined from 51 to 48 species in unfenced plots. On average, only 28% of species that were present in the fenced plots (mean no. species = 10.4) were present in the unfenced plots.

Over all years, the number of fenced and unfenced plots containing exotic species exhibited similar changes observed for overall species richness. In general, exotic species were present in more fenced plots than in unfenced plots and individual fenced plots contained more exotic species than did individual unfenced plots. Twenty-two of the 24 exotic species recorded from plots have been present in at least one fenced plot during one or more of the four sampling periods. Since 1995, two species were first observed in fenced plots in 1998 and two species were first observed in fenced plots in 2003. The overall increase in the number of exotic species in plots between 1993 and 2003 is due solely to an increase observed in fenced plots on Mount Joy (from 78 to 95 [number of species occurrences per plot summed over all the plots]).

Mean tree seedling counts in 2003 were greater in fenced plots, but the large variability in seedling counts among plots precluded any statistically significant evidence of a change over time or differences between Mount Joy and Mount Misery. By 2003, there were, on average, 7.1 (SE=1.56) and 11.3 (SE=1.54) more species of tree seedlings in fenced plots than in unfenced plots on Mount Misery and Mount Joy, respectively.

Guidelines for acceptable abundance of tree seedlings for forest regeneration are 25 seedlings per 12.57 m$^2$ (135 ft$^2$ [McWilliams et al. 2002]). The percentage of plots with adequate seedling abundance is referred to as a stocking rate. We calculated stocking rates using all tree species combined, only native tree species, and only deer-preferred tree species. When either exotic tree species or species that deer do not prefer are excluded from the calculations there was minimal effect on stocking rates. In 1993, three percent of both unfenced and fenced plots had adequate seedling abundance. However, by 2003 the stocking rate in fenced and unfenced plots was 27% and 0%, respectively.

In 2003, four (Jack-in-the-pulpit [*Arisaema triphyllum*], wild sarsaparilla [*Aralia nudicaulis*], sweet cicely [*Osmorhiza claytoni*], and Indian cucumber root [*Medeola virginiana*]) of six herbaceous species known to occur in the park that have been proposed as potential indicator species of the effects of deer browsing (Latham et al. 2005) occurred in nine of 30 fenced plots (1–3 species present per plot), and one species (Jack-in-the-pulpit) was present in six of 30 unfenced plots. Whenever Jack-in-the-pulpit was present in an unfenced plot, it also occurred in the paired fenced plot.

# Acknowledgments

We thank Margaret A. Carfioli for assistance with explaining the data collection methods and providing assistance with use of the database. Also, we thank the National Park Service for letting us use contents from the report on the analysis of 1993–1998 data vegetation.

# Introduction

A fixed-plot monitoring system (Storm and Ross 1992) was implemented in 1992 to evaluate vegetative communities in two large wooded areas at Valley Forge National Historical Park. The objectives of this monitoring system are to:

1. Describe the existing understory plant community on Mount Misery and Mount Joy in terms of species richness and abundance; and

2. Determine changes in abundance and species composition of understory plant communities in fenced and unfenced plots over time.

Data collected at four time periods (1993, 1995–1996, 1998, and 2003) as part of this monitoring program were provided in a Microsoft Access database. We analyzed these data to statistically test if changes in the vegetation occurred over time.

## Study Area

### Regional Information

Valley Forge National Historical Park is located 20 km (12.4 mi) northwest of Philadelphia, Pennsylvania in Chester and Montgomery counties, within the Upland Piedmont Plateau ecological region in southeastern Pennsylvania (Keys et al. 1995). The park consists of 1,403 ha (3,466 ac). It is located just south of Braun's (1950) boundary between the Glaciated and Piedmont sections of the Oak-Chestnut Forest Region, which also approximates the boundary between the Lowland and Upland U.S. Forest Service subsections of the Piedmont (Kasmer et al. 1994; Keys et al. 1995). The area has a long history of human impacts from forest clearing for encampment during the Revolutionary War (1777–1778), agriculture, industrial use, and development. All of these factors, in addition to the bedrock geology, soil composition, and site-specific characteristics, such as slope, aspect, and moisture regime, influence the current-day vegetation patterns at Valley Forge NHP (Podniesinski et al. 2005).

### Park-specific Information

The two largest contiguous park woodlands, Mount Misery and Mount Joy, were selected as sample polygons. Large sections of each polygon bordering Valley Creek have slopes >15 degrees and were excluded from the sampling polygon. Mount Misery borders Valley Creek to the west and encompasses approximately 93 ha (229 ac). Mount Joy borders Valley Creek to the east and encompasses approximately 94 ha (233 ac).

### Vegetation

The predominant existing forest communities at Valley Forge National Historical Park include a Dry Oak Forest that occurs primarily on ridges and slopes of Mount Misery and Mount Joy, and a Successional Tuliptree Forest that occurs on the lower slopes and flat terrain. The Dry Oak community covers approximately 158 ha (390 ac) and the Successional Tuliptree community covers approximately 151 ha (374 ac) of the park (Davis et al. 2006).

The Dry Oak Forest type is most common on the slopes of Mount Joy and Mount Misery within the park. The canopy is dominated by drought-tolerant chestnut oak (*Quercus prinus*) and black oak (*Quercus veluntina*) with blackgum (*Nyssa sylvatica*) and scarlet oak (*Quercus coccinea*) as occasional codominants. The subcanopy is characterized by moderate to dense cover of blackgum, red maple (*Acer rubrum*), and sassafras (*Sassafras albidum*). The tall shrub layer is often diagnostic for this type, characterized by moderate to dense cover of mountain laurel (*Kalmia latifolia*). In some stands, the tall-shrub layer is dominated by young blackgum. Also common in the tall-shrub layer are red maple, sassafras, and witch-hazel (*Hamamelis virginiana*). The low-shrub and herbaceous layers are typically very sparse or absent, presumably due to heavy deer browse. The low-shrub layer, when present, is limited to seedlings of canopy trees and a few ericaceous species: early lowbush blueberry (*Vaccinium pallidum*), black huckleberry (*Gaylussacia baccata*), and pink azalea (*Rhododendron periclymenoides*). Herbaceous plants typically occur as solitary individuals or small clumps, when present. Common herbaceous species include striped pipsissewa (*Chimaphila maculata*), hay-scented fern (*Dennstaedtia punctilobula*), marginal woodfern (*Dryopteris marginalis*), and Indian cucumber-root (*Medeola virginiana*).

The mesic variant of the Dry Oak Forest (Podniesinski et al. 2005) occurs on moderate slopes with slightly more mesic soils than is found on the upper slopes. Canopy dominants are dry-site oaks (chestnut oak, black oak, and scarlet oak), but the canopy also includes a greater proportion of other hardwood species, including white oak (*Quercus alba*), red maple, tuliptree (*Lirodendron tulipifera*), American beech (*Fagus grandifolia*), and sassafras. A subcanopy is usually present, characterized by a mix of hardwood species such as red maple, sassafras, American beech, chestnut oak, and black oak. Typical tall shrubs include flowering dogwood (*Cornus florida*), witch-hazel, and mountain laurel. The tall-shrub layer varies from sparse to abundant, with flowering dogwood exceeding 50% cover in some locations. The low-shrub and herbaceous layers are very sparse to nearly absent, presumably the result of intense deer browse. The low-shrub layer is characterized by seedlings of the canopy and subcanopy woody species. Typical herbaceous species include garlic mustard (*Alliaria petiolata*), Japanese stiltgrass (*Microstegium vimineum*), and Pennsylvania sedge (*Carex pensylvanica*).

The Successional Tuliptree Forest community occurs throughout the park on a variety of substrates and soil types. This forest community occurs as mid-successional and mature forest stands. Some of these stands were planted 70 to 80 years ago. The most characteristic feature of this community type is the dominance of tuliptree. Tuliptree is the only dominant in many stands, with black oak and white ash (*Fraxinus americana*) codominant or subdominant in others. Other occasional canopy trees include red maple, northern red oak, and sassafras. The subcanopy is usually open (typically less than 30% total cover, though may approach 50%), characterized by tuliptree, red maple, tall individuals of flowering dogwood, blackgum, occasional redbud (*Cercis canadensis*), and sassafras. The shrub layer is also open and appears to be pruned below 1.5 m (5 ft) by heavy deer browse. Typical shrub species are flowering dogwood (clear dominant in the shrub layer), northern spicebush (*Lindera benzoin*), mountain laurel, and the nonnative Japanese honeysuckle (*Lonicera japonica*). Smooth blackhaw (*Viburnum prunifolium*) also occurs sporadically. The herbaceous layer has very low diversity and is dominated by exotics, including Japanese stiltgrass, except in stands with a very dense canopy, in which case there may be a high proportion of bare ground. Other herbaceous associates in addition to Japanese stiltgrass include garlic mustard, Oriental lady's-thumb (*Polygonum caespitosum*), Jack-in-the-pulpit (*Arisaema triphyllum*), and Canadian clearweed (*Pilea pumila*). Characteristic species that occur in the Successional Tuliptree Forest community, and that do not typically occur in the oak forests, include hairy Solomon's-seal (*Polygonatum pubescens*), Maryland black snakeroot (*Sanicula marilandica*), and alpine enchanter's nightshade (*Circaea alpina*).

Substrate

Mount Misery consists of the Cambrian Age Chickies Formation, a very hard, erosion-resistant rock composed of quartzite and quartz schist. Dry Oak Forests dominated by chestnut oak, black oak, northern red oak, and white oak are common on these acidic, well-drained, rocky Edgemont soils occurring on upper slopes (USDA SCS 1967). The infertile soils and the steep terrain on Mount Misery were likely unsuitable for farming historically. The forests on this ridge were used as woodlots for charcoal production (Rhoads et al. 1989).

Mount Joy occurs on the slightly younger Cambrian Age Antietam and Harpers (undivided) formations. These rock types are composed of quartzite, schist, and phyllite, and are fairly erosion resistant. Edgemont stony loam soils derived from these formations can be somewhat calcareous and are slightly more mesic than soils that occur on the Chickies Quartzite Formation (Pennsylvania Geological Survey 1981; Pennsylvania Bureau of Topographic and Geographic Survey 2001; Podniesinski et al. 2005). These moderate slopes may have been better suited for farming historically than the steeper slopes and rockier soils of Mount Misery (Rhoads et al. 1989). The Successional Tuliptree community is common on these substrates as well as those derived from the Triassic Stockton Formation.

Methods

Plot Selection

Thirty vegetation sample sites were located on Mount Misery and Mount Joy (15 in each area). These vegetation sample sites were selected randomly by overlaying a grid (cell size = 36.5 m² [383.2 ft²]) on a map of the study area. Grid intersections (representing the center of each potential sample site) were randomly selected as sample sites. If a selected sample site was located on a trail, road, park boundary, or had a slope of >50%, another site was randomly selected.

A 3×3 m (9.8×9.8 ft) fenced area was established with its center at each randomly located grid intersection in May and June 1992 (Figure 1). The boundaries of fenced vegetation areas were oriented along cardinal directions. The corners of each fenced area were marked with galvanized metal posts (2 m [6.5 ft] in height), and metal fencing (12.5 gauge, 2 m [6.5 ft] in height) was secured to the posts with aluminum ties. Fencing mesh size was 5×10 cm (1.96×3.94 in) to allow entry of small rodents such as eastern gray squirrel (*Sciurus carolinensis*), eastern chipmunk (*Tamias striatus*), and cottontail rabbits (*Sylvilagus floridanus*), but exclude white-tailed deer (*Odocoileus virginianus*). A 2×2 m (6.5×6.5 ft) plot centered within the fenced area was used for vegetation sampling.

The centers of thirty 2×2 m (6.5×6.5 ft) unfenced control plots (15 in each area) were located 36.5 m (383.2 ft [one grid cell]) from fenced plot centers in a randomly selected cardinal direction. Unfenced plots were selected based on the similarity of ecological attributes (soil type, aspect, slope, geological substrate, hydrologic features, and forest type) to the corresponding fenced plot to provide matched, paired plots. Ninety percent (*n*=27) of unfenced plots were established 36.5 m (383.2 ft) from fenced plot centers. The remaining unfenced plots (*n*=3) were established 20–27.4 m (65.6–89.9 ft) from the center of the corresponding fenced plot in order to maintain a similarity of ecological attributes. The center of each unfenced plot was marked with a galvanized metal post (2 m [6.5 ft] in height).

Vegetation Sampling

Plots were sampled in 1993, 1995–96, 1998, and 2003; however, because most data from the 1995–96 sampling period occurred in 1995, we treated data from plots sampled in 1996 as if they were sampled in 1995. The vegetative community in the 3×3 m (9.8×9.8 ft) fenced areas was measured within a central 2×2 m (6.5×6.5 ft) plot delineated with a 4-m² (43-ft²) PVC frame. Walking within fenced sites was restricted to the buffer surrounding the area sampled. Vegetation sampling of unfenced plots was similarly restricted to the 2×2 m (6.5×6.5 ft) area surrounding the metal center post. The PVC frame was oriented along cardinal directions with the post of the unfenced plot in the center of the frame.

The classification of vegetative species as herbaceous, vine, or shrub was based on Rhoads and Klein (1993). In 2003, additional references were used to confirm species classifications and update taxonomy: Pennsylvania Flora Project database (http://www.paflora.org/), U.S. Department of Agriculture PLANTS database (http://plants.usda.gov/index.html), and the U.S. Department of Agriculture ITIS database (http://www.itis.usda.gov/advanced_search.html). Tree

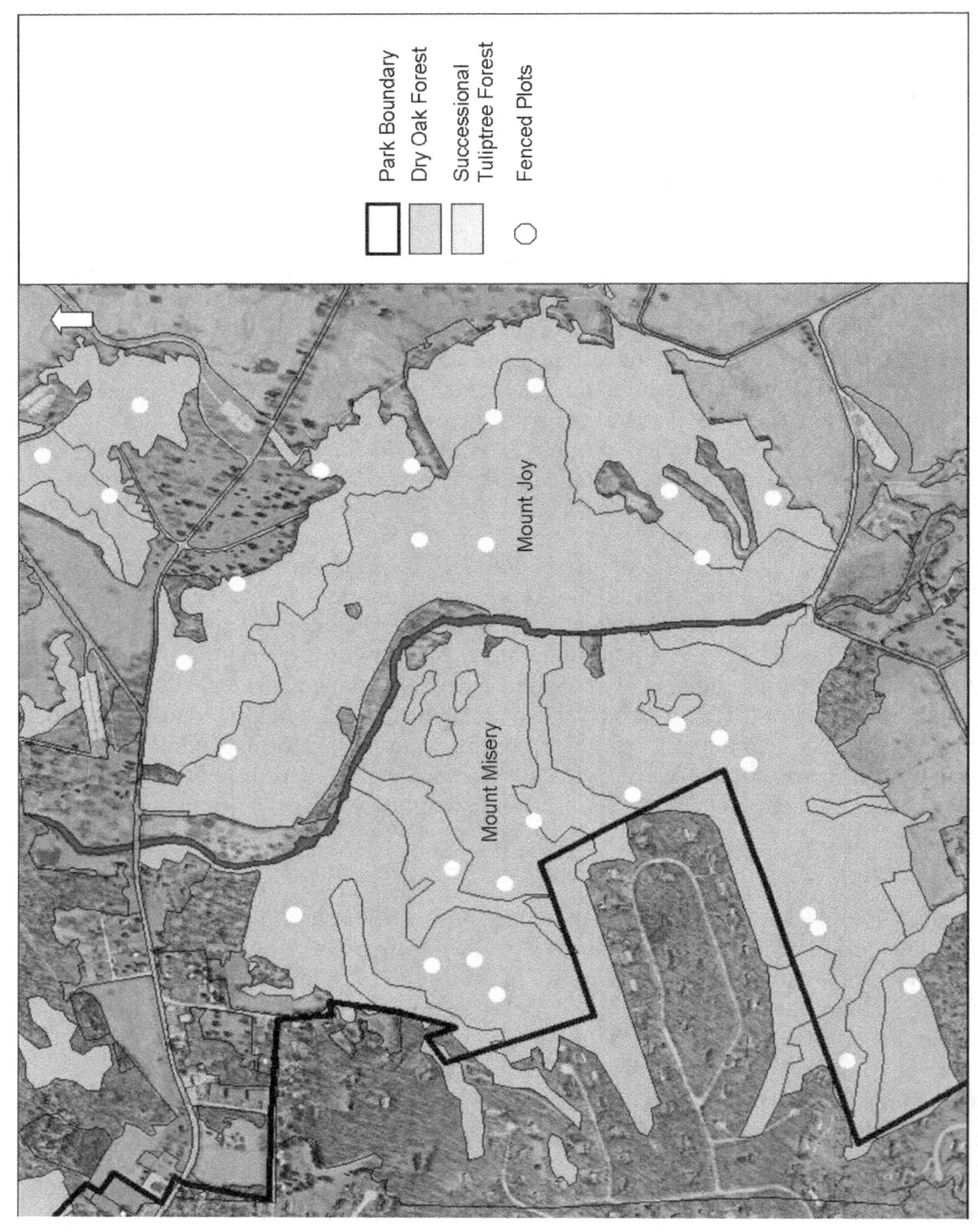

Figure 1. Location of fenced monitoring plots with in Dry Oak Forest and Successional Tuliptree Forest types on Mount Misery and Mount Joy, Valley Forge National Historical Park, Pennsylvania.

seedlings were classified as stems $\leq 150$ cm (60 in) in height. Measurement of vegetation followed as closely as possible protocols developed by Storm and Ross (1992) for monitoring vegetation on public lands in Mid-Atlantic States. However, changes in protocols occurred over the years because of time and personnel constraints.

Herbaceous, Shrub, and Vine Cover: 1993 and 1995

Herbaceous vegetation, shrubs, and vines were typically identified to species, and minimally to genus. For each species, a visual estimate of percent cover within a plot was recorded in the following classes: 1=0–4%; 2=5–25%; 3=26–50%; 4=51–75%; 5=76–95%; and 6=96–100%. Vegetation was not stratified by height.

Herbaceous, Shrub, and Vine Cover: 1998

Data were collected as in 1993 and 1995. In addition, each 2×2 m (6.5×6.5 ft) plot was divided into four 1×1 m (3.25×3.25 ft) quadrants in 1998 and at the center of each quadrant mean height of all herbaceous, shrub, and vine species combined was estimated. A visual estimate of percent vegetation cover (all herbaceous, shrub, and vine species combined) within each 2×2 m (6.5×6.5 ft) sample plot also was recorded. All plants in 1998 were identified to species.

Herbaceous, Shrub, and Vine Cover: 2003

Data were collected as in 1993 and 1995. In addition, when it was easy to determine that shrub stems were present within one height class, the height class of shrubs was recorded using the same height classes used for tree seedlings (1=0–25 cm, 2=26–50 cm, 3=51–75 cm, 4=76–100 cm, 5=101–125 cm, and 6=126–150 cm). When shrubs were distributed through multiple height classes, the height of the majority of the shrub cover was recorded in one of the following two height classes, $\leq 100$ cm ($\leq 39.4$ in) or >100–150 cm (>39.4–59.0 in).

Tree seedlings: 1993, 1995, 1998, and 2003

All tree seedlings in each 2×2 m (6.5×6.5 ft) vegetation plot were identified to species (except *Carya* sp. in 1998), counted, and recorded by height class. Tree seedling height classes were defined as follows: 1=0–25 cm (0–9.8 in); 2=26–50 cm (10.2–19.7 in); 3=51–75 cm (20.0–29.5 in); 4=76–100 cm (29.9–39.4 in); 5=101–125 cm (39.7–49.2 in); and 6=126–150 cm (49.6–59.0 in).

Statistical Methods

Species richness

We used repeated measures ANOVA to test whether differences in species richness between fenced and unfenced plots occurred over time. We used PROC GLM in SAS 9.1 (SAS Institute, Inc. 2003) with the REPEATED statement to conduct the repeated measures analysis, in which the dependent variable was the difference in number of species between paired fenced and unfenced plots. We considered differences between fenced and unfenced plots ($n$=30) as subjects with repeated measurements over time modeled using an orthogonal polynomial transformation, in which the spacing of the orthogonal polynomials was the number of years since 1993 the data were collected (i.e., 0 years for data collected in 1993, 2 for 1995, 5 for 1998, and 10 for 2003). An additional factor in the analysis was site (Mount Joy or Mount Misery). We used MANOVA test criteria and exact F statistics to test hypotheses of time and interaction effects ($\alpha=0.05$).

Some taxa were classified only to genera (i.e., *Carex, Carya, Eupatorium, Smilax, Polygonatum,* and *Vaccinium*) because classification to species did not occur across all years of data collection. Also, using only 2003 data, we calculated the percentage of species that were present in the fenced plots that were also present in the unfenced plots. We summarized these results by plot, by forest stand, and across all plots.

Tree seedling abundance

We used the same repeated measures ANOVA analysis to test whether changes in stem density of all tree seedling species occurred over time, and whether density differed between fenced and unfenced plots.

Principal Components Analysis

We conducted a principal components analysis (PROC PRINCOMP [SAS Institute, Inc. 2003]), in which the analysis used the number of plants (or presence) by plant type (herbaceous, vine, shrub, and tree) on each plot. We used only data from 2003 and analyzed Mount Joy and Mount Misery data separately. We plotted the principal component scores from the first two eigenvectors to illustrate differences between fenced and unfenced plots. These plots provide a means of assessing how fenced and unfenced plots differed according to plant counts (or presence) by plant type.

Stocking rates

Guidelines for acceptable abundance of tree seedlings and small saplings for forest regeneration are 25 seedlings per 12.57 m$^2$ (135.3 ft$^2$) (McWilliams et al. 2002), in which weights are applied according to height class (Table 1). The percentage of plots with adequate seedling abundance is referred to as a stocking rate. Any combination of weighted stem counts $\geq25$ seedlings/12.57 m$^2$ (135.3 ft$^2$) is considered adequate stocking.

Stem count data collected at Valley Forge National Historical Park included only tree species seedlings up to 150 cm in height and were recorded in slightly different height classes (Table 2). We weighted these height classes as closely as possibly to those defined by McWilliams et al. (2002) and corrected for the different sized sampling areas. Seedlings <5.1 cm (<2 in) in height should not be included in calculating stocking rates because most of these individuals do not survive; therefore, we assigned seedlings in the >0–25 cm (>0–9.8 in) class a weight of zero. Also, we were missing the last two height classes used by McWilliams et al. (2002). Using the revised criteria, we calculated stocking rates for all tree species, only native tree species, and only deer-preferred tree species. Exotic tree species excluded for the analysis of native tree species were Norway maple (*Acer platanoides*), tree of heaven (*Ailanthus altissima*), princess tree (*Paulownia tomentosa*), and sweet cherry (*Prunus avium*) (see Appendix A).

Table 1.  Height classes of tree seedlings and small saplings and assigned weights from U.S. Forest Service, Forest Inventory Analysis (McWilliams et al. 2002), used to calculate stocking rates of advanced forest regeneration.

| Height class | Weight |
|---|---|
| 5.1–14.7 cm | 1 |
| >14.7–30.0 cm | 1 |
| >30–90 cm | 2 |
| >90–150 cm | 20 |
| >150–310 cm | 50 |
| >310 cm and <12.5 cm dbh | 50 |

Table 2.  Height classes of tree seedlings used at Valley Forge National Historical Park, 1993–2003, and assigned weights for calculating stocking rates of advanced forest regeneration.

| Height class | Weight |
|---|---|
| >0–25 cm | 0 |
| >25–50 cm | 1 |
| >50–75 cm | 2 |
| >75–100 cm | 2 |
| >100–125 cm | 20 |
| >125–150 cm | 20 |

Indicator species

There are several herbaceous species that have been suggested as indicators of deer browsing intensity (Latham et al. 2005).  The species that occur in Valley Forge National Historical Park are Jack-in-the-pulpit (*Arisaema triphyllum*), wild sarsaparilla (*Aralia nudicaulis*), sweet cicely (*Osmorhiza claytoni*), Indian cucumber root (*Medeola virginiana*), *Trillium* spp., white wood aster (*Symphyotrichum divaricatum*), and jewelweed (*Impatiens capensis*).  However, we excluded jewelweed because is it strongly associated with riparian habitats and would likely require a different sampling scheme to be adequately represented in samples.  We summarized which of these species were present in fenced and unfenced plots.

Results

## Species Richness

We did not distinguish between native and exotic species in our analysis of species richness because excluding or including exotic species had no effect on the results. The repeated measures ANOVA indicated that species richness increased over time ($F_{3,26}=6.27$, $P=0.002$) in fenced plots on both Mount Misery and Mount Joy. In unfenced plots, species richness exhibited no change or a slight decline over time in both areas (Table 3, Figure 2). Species richness was greater on Mount Joy but differences in species richness between fenced and unfenced plots were similar for both areas ($F_{1,28}=3.19$, $P=0.085$), and differences between areas did not change over time ($F_{3,26}=1.14$, $P=0.350$). From 1993 to 2003 on Mount Misery, the total number of species increased 32% (from 31 to 41 species) in fenced plots, and decreased 15% (from 27 to 23 species) in unfenced plots (Appendixes B–E). On Mount Joy, the total number of species increased 27% (from 56 to 71 species) in fenced plots and declined 6% (from 51 to 48 species) in unfenced plots.

By 2003, on average over both sites, only 28% of species that were present in the fenced plots (average no. species in fenced plots = 10.4) were present in the unfenced plots (Table 4). The Mount Misery area averaged 34% (average no. species in fenced plots = 8.0), whereas the Mount Joy area averaged 23% (average no. species in fenced plots = 12.8). The average number of species in unfenced plots that were not found in the paired fenced plots on Mount Misery and Mount Joy was 1.5 and 2.9, respectively.

Over all years, the number of fenced and unfenced plots containing exotic species exhibited similar changes observed for overall species richness. In general, exotic species were present in more fenced plots than in unfenced plots, and individual fenced plots contained more exotic species than did individual unfenced plots. Twenty-two of the 24 exotic species recorded from plots have been present in at least one fenced plot during one or more of the four sampling periods (Table 5). Two species were first observed in fenced plots in 1998 and two species were first observed in fenced plots in 2003. The overall increase in the occurrence of exotic species in plots between 1993 and 2003 is due solely to an increase observed on fenced plots on Mount Joy (78 to 95 plots [number of occurrences per plot summed over all the plots]).

Table 3. Average number of species present in fenced and unfenced plots on Mount Misery and Mount Joy, Valley Forge National Historical Park, Pennsylvania, 1993–2003.

| | Mount Misery | | | | Mount Joy | | | |
| | Fenced | | Unfenced | | Fenced | | Unfenced | |
| Year | $\bar{x}$ | 95% CI | $\bar{x}$ | 95% CI | $\bar{x}$ | 95% CI | $\bar{x}$ | 95% CI |
|---|---|---|---|---|---|---|---|---|
| 1993 | 6.7 | 5.2–8.2 | 5.1 | 3.7–6.4 | 9.4 | 6.4–12.4 | 7.2 | 4.8–9.6 |
| 1995 | 7.4 | 5.6–9.2 | 4.9 | 3.5–6.3 | 10.9 | 7.4–14.4 | 5.9 | 3.2–8.7 |
| 1998 | 8.3 | 6.3–10.2 | 4.4 | 3.0–5.7 | 11.4 | 8.6–14.2 | 5.2 | 2.7–7.7 |
| 2003 | 8.0 | 5.7–10.3 | 3.9 | 2.8–5.1 | 12.8 | 9.9–15.7 | 5.9 | 3.5–8.3 |

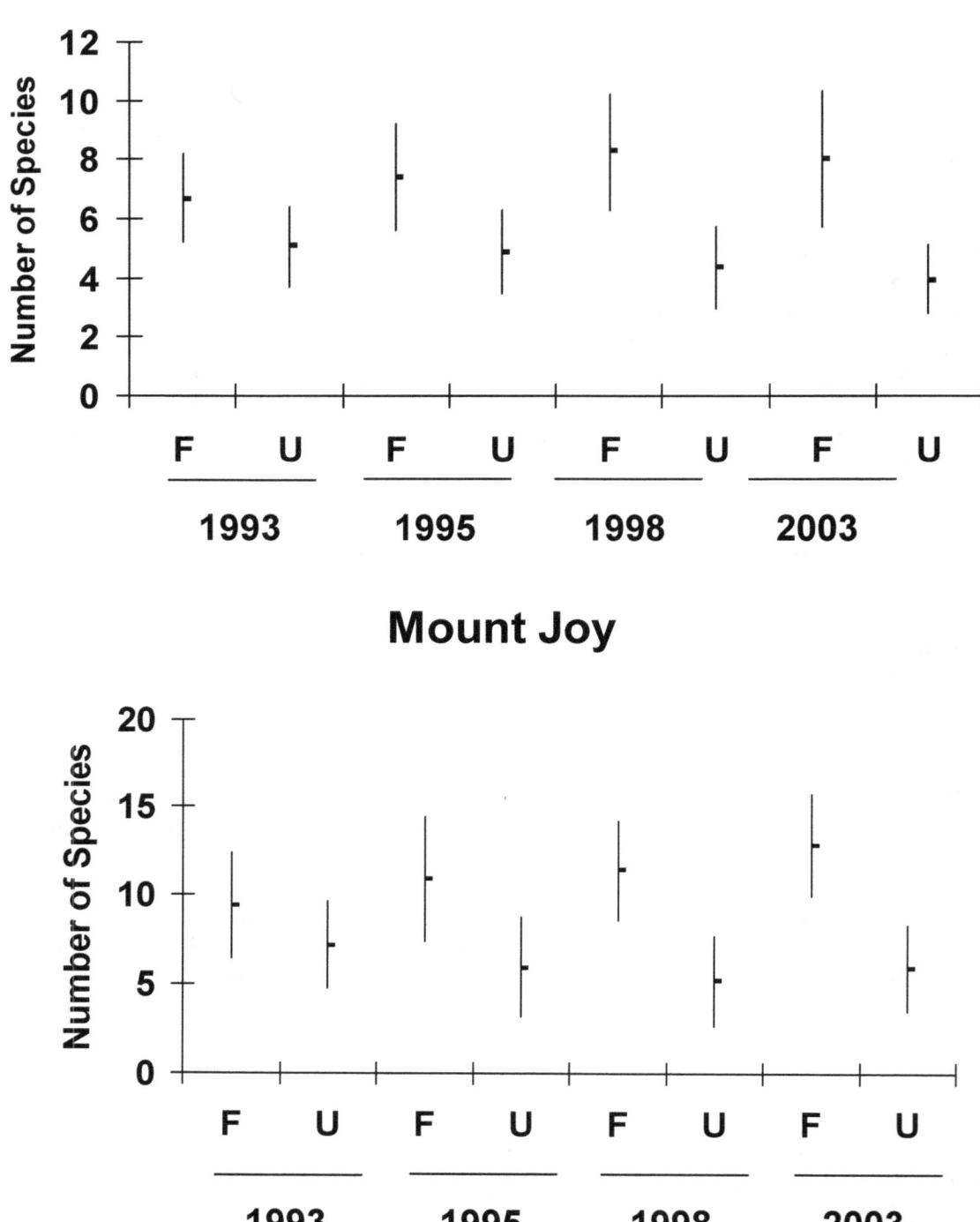

Figure 2. Average number of species found in fenced (F) and unfenced (U) plots on Mount Misery and Mount Joy during 1993, 1995, 1998, and 2003, Valley Forge National Historical Park, Pennsylvania.

Table 4. Number of species present in fenced plots and percentage of these species present in the paired unfenced plots on Mount Misery and Mount Joy, Valley Forge National Historical Park, Pennsylvania, 2003.

| Area | Site No. | No. of Species Present in Fenced Plot | Percent of Species Present in Fenced Plot also Present in Unfenced Plot |
|------|----------|------|------|
| Mount Misery | 1 | 9 | 33 |
| | 2 | 6 | 0 |
| | 3 | 3 | 33 |
| | 4 | 9 | 33 |
| | 5 | 3 | 33 |
| | 6 | 15 | 7 |
| | 7 | 13 | 31 |
| | 8 | 7 | 29 |
| | 9 | 13 | 23 |
| | 10 | 7 | 29 |
| | 11 | 10 | 50 |
| | 12 | 3 | 67 |
| | 13 | 6 | 33 |
| | 14 | 13 | 38 |
| | 15 | 3 | 67 |
| Mount Joy | 16 | 25 | 44 |
| | 17 | 18 | 22 |
| | 18 | 6 | 17 |
| | 19 | 14 | 36 |
| | 20 | 12 | 17 |
| | 21 | 16 | 6 |
| | 22 | 9 | 22 |
| | 23 | 17 | 6 |
| | 24 | 12 | 8 |
| | 25 | 18 | 17 |
| | 26 | 5 | 40 |
| | 27 | 8 | 38 |
| | 28 | 12 | 50 |
| | 29 | 11 | 9 |
| | 30 | 9 | 11 |

Table 5. Number of fenced and unfenced plots containing exotic species on Mount Misery and Mount Joy, Valley Forge National Historical Park, Pennsylvania, 1993–2003.

| Area and Treatment | Scientific name | Common name | Plant Type | 1993 | 1995 | 1998 | 2003 |
|---|---|---|---|---|---|---|---|
| Mount Misery | | | | | | | |
| fenced | *Polygonum caespitosum* | smartweed | herb | 0 | 0 | 0 | 1 |
| fenced | *Prunus avium* | sweet cherry | tree | 0 | 0 | 1 | 0 |
| fenced | *Lonicera japonica* | Japanese honeysuckle | vine | 1 | 0 | 0 | 0 |
| fenced | *Polygonum aviculare* | knotweed | herb | 1 | 0 | 1 | 0 |
| fenced | *Celastrus orbiculatus* | oriental bittersweet | vine | 1 | 1 | 0 | 0 |
| fenced | *Microstegium vimineum* | stilt grass | herb | 3 | 0 | 0 | 0 |
| Total species occurrences – fenced plots | | | | 6 | 1 | 2 | 1 |
| Mount Misery (continued) | | | | | | | |
| unfenced | *Berberis thunbergii* | Japanese Barberry | shrub | 0 | 0 | 1 | 0 |
| unfenced | *Celastrus orbiculatus* | oriental bittersweet | vine | 0 | 0 | 1 | 0 |
| unfenced | *Microstegium vimineum* | stilt grass | herb | 1 | 1 | 0 | 0 |
| Total species occurrences – unfenced plots | | | | 1 | 1 | 2 | 0 |
| Total species occurrences – Mount Misery | | | | 7 | 2 | 4 | 1 |
| Mount Joy | | | | | | | |
| fenced | *Ailanthus altissima* | tree of heaven | tree | 0 | 0 | 0 | 2 |
| fenced | *Euonymus alata* | burning bush | shrub | 0 | 0 | 0 | 4 |
| fenced | *Lonicera morrowii* | morrow honeysuckle | shrub | 0 | 0 | 1 | 3 |
| fenced | *Polygonum aviculare* | knotweed | herb | 0 | 0 | 3 | 0 |
| fenced | *Lonicera maackii* | amur honeysuckle | shrub | 0 | 0 | 3 | 7 |
| fenced | *Paulownia tomentosa* | princess tree | tree | 0 | 1 | 0 | 0 |
| fenced | *Rhodotypos scandens* | jetbead | shrub | 0 | 1 | 1 | 1 |
| fenced | *Rosa multiflora* | multiflora rose | shrub | 0 | 1 | 1 | 1 |
| fenced | *Acer platanoides* | Norway maple | tree | 0 | 2 | 1 | 4 |
| fenced | *Berberis thunbergii* | Japanese barberry | shrub | 1 | 0 | 0 | 0 |
| fenced | *Cardamine impatiens* | bitter-cress | herb | 1 | 0 | 1 | 1 |
| fenced | *Prunus avium* | sweet cherry | tree | 1 | 0 | 4 | 1 |
| fenced | *Ligustrum vulgare* | common privet | shrub | 1 | 1 | 2 | 8 |
| fenced | *Duchesnea indica* | indian strawberry | herb | 2 | 0 | 1 | 0 |
| fenced | *Alliaria petiolata* | garlic-mustard | herb | 2 | 0 | 6 | 7 |
| fenced | *Lonicera japonica* | Japanese honeysuckle | vine | 2 | 7 | 4 | 5 |
| fenced | *Rubus phoenicolasius* | wineberry | shrub | 3 | 2 | 2 | 6 |
| fenced | *Pastinaca sativa* | wild parsnip | herb | 3 | 3 | 0 | 0 |
| fenced | *Celastrus orbiculatus* | oriental bittersweet | vine | 5 | 5 | 8 | 7 |
| fenced | *Polygonum caespitosum* | smartweed | herb | 6 | 3 | 0 | 2 |
| fenced | *Microstegium vimineum* | stilt grass | herb | 6 | 3 | 2 | 5 |
| fenced | *Malva neglecta* | common mallow | herb | 6 | 4 | 0 | 0 |
| Total species occurrences – fenced plots | | | | 39 | 33 | 40 | 64 |
| unfenced | *Ligustrum vulgare* | common privet | shrub | 0 | 0 | 0 | 1 |
| unfenced | *Ranunculus bulbosus* | bulbous buttercup | herb | 0 | 0 | 0 | 1 |
| unfenced | *Taraxacum officinale* | common dandelion | herb | 0 | 0 | 0 | 1 |
| unfenced | *Euonymus alata* | burning bush | shrub | 0 | 0 | 0 | 2 |
| unfenced | *Lonicera maackii* | amur honeysuckle | shrub | 0 | 0 | 0 | 3 |
| unfenced | *Acer platanoides* | Norway maple | tree | 0 | 1 | 0 | 0 |
| unfenced | *Polygonum aviculare* | knotweed | herb | 0 | 1 | 4 | 1 |
| unfenced | *Cardamine impatiens* | bitter-cress | herb | 1 | 1 | 1 | 1 |
| unfenced | *Alliaria petiolata* | garlic-mustard | herb | 1 | 1 | 5 | 3 |
| unfenced | *Prunus avium* | sweet cherry | tree | 2 | 0 | 0 | 0 |
| unfenced | *Duchesnea indica* | Indian strawberry | herb | 2 | 2 | 2 | 1 |
| unfenced | *Pastinaca sativa* | wild parsnip | herb | 3 | 2 | 0 | 0 |
| unfenced | *Lonicera japonica* | Jap. honeysuckle | vine | 3 | 4 | 2 | 2 |

Table 5. Number of plots containing exotic species in fenced and unfenced plots on Mount Misery and Mount Joy, Valley Forge National Historical Park, Pennsylvania, 1993–2003 (continued).

| Area and Treatment | Scientific name | Common name | Plant Type | 1993 | 1995 | 1998 | 2003 |
|---|---|---|---|---|---|---|---|
| Mount Joy (cont'd.) | | | | | | | |
| unfenced | *Microstegium vimineum* | stilt grass | herb | 4 | 6 | 8 | 7 |
| unfenced | *Malva neglecta* | common mallow | herb | 5 | 7 | 0 | 0 |
| unfenced | *Celastrus orbiculatus* | oriental bittersweet | vine | 5 | 7 | 5 | 2 |
| unfenced | *Rubus phoenicolasius* | wineberry | shrub | 6 | 2 | 2 | 2 |
| unfenced | *Polygonum caespitosum* | smartweed | herb | 7 | 3 | 1 | 4 |
| Total species occurrences – unfenced plots | | | | 39 | 37 | 30 | 31 |
| Total species occurrences – Mount Joy | | | | 78 | 70 | 70 | 95 |

The number of plots containing at least one exotic species changed little over time in either site or in fenced and unfenced plots. On Mount Misery, between 1993 and 2003, the number of fenced plots with at least one exotic species declined from five plots to one plot and unfenced plots with at least one exotic species decreased from one plot to zero plots. On Mount Joy, between 1993 and 2003, the number of fenced plots with at least one exotic species increased from ten plots to 12 plots, and the number of unfenced plots containing at least one exotic species decreased from 11 plots to nine plots.

Tree Seedling Abundance

We failed to detect a change in seedling counts between fenced and unfenced plots over time ($F_{3,26}=2.23$, $P=0.109$) or between Mount Joy and Mount Misery ($F_{3,26}=0.37$, $P=0.547$), or an interaction between time and areas ($F_{3,26}=1.14$, $P=0.351$). However, there was some evidence of an increase in seedling counts over time because a univariate test of the hypothesis of no time effect was rejected ($F_{3,84}=3.67$, Huyn-Feldt $P=0.041$). Both areas had increasing mean counts of seedlings, but the variability was large (Table 6, Figure 3).

By 2003, on Mount Misery there were 7.1 (SE=1.56) more species of tree seedlings, on average, in fenced plots than in unfenced plots. On Mount Joy by 2003, on average, there were 11.3 (SE=1.54) more species in fenced plots than in unfenced plots. Average number of seedlings and standard deviation by species, height class, fencing treatment, and area are presented in Table 7. Pooling seedling counts across species, but not height classes, indicated that in unfenced plots no seedlings were found taller than height class 1 on either Mount Misery or Mount Joy (Table 8).

Table 6. Average number of tree seedlings present in fenced and unfenced plots on Mount Misery and Mount Joy, Valley Forge National Historical Park, Pennsylvania, 1993–2003.

| | Mount Misery | | | | Mount Joy | | | |
| | Fenced | | Unfenced | | Fenced | | Unfenced | |
| Year | $\bar{x}$ | 95% CI | $\bar{x}$ | 95% CI | $\bar{x}$ | 95% CI | $\bar{x}$ | 95% CI |
|---|---|---|---|---|---|---|---|---|
| 1993 | 17.7 | 8.4–27.0 | 11.8 | 3.9–19.7 | 6.5 | 2.0–10.9 | 3.7 | 1.1–6.2 |
| 1995 | 21.7 | 8.9–34.4 | 10.0 | 2.8–17.2 | 12.6 | 4.1–21.1 | 4.2 | -2.1–10.5 |
| 1998 | 24.7 | 10.4–39.1 | 8.3 | 1.6–15.0 | 10.8 | 4.1–17.5 | 3.5 | -1.4–8.8 |
| 2003 | 26.0 | 10.1–41.9 | 9.3 | 5.0–13.5 | 24.1 | 6.7–41.5 | 9.7 | 0.7–18.8 |

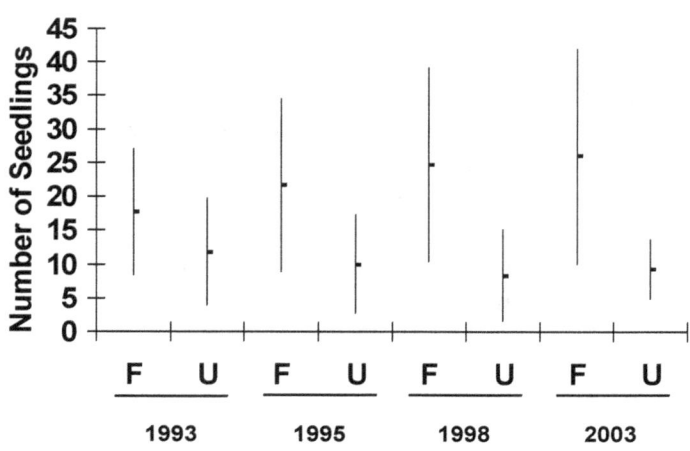

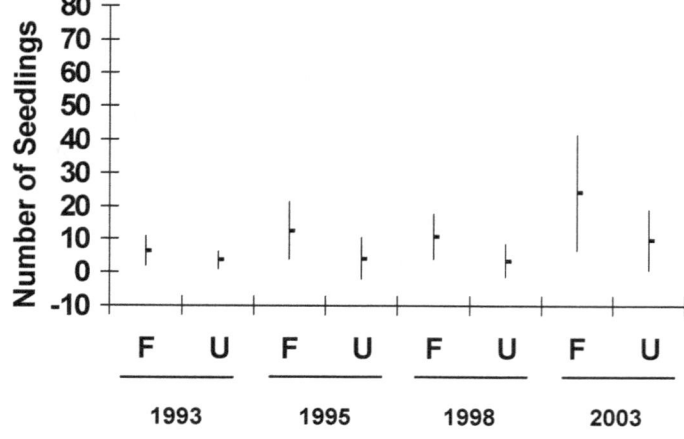

Figure 3. Average number of tree seedlings found on fenced (F) and unfenced (U) plots on Mount Misery and Mount Joy during 1993, 1995, 1998, and 2003, Valley Forge National Historical Park, Pennsylvania.

Table 7. Average number of tree seedlings per plot and standard deviation (SD), by species and height class, for Mount Joy and Mount Misery, Valley Forge National Historical Park, Pennsylvania, 2003.

| | | Mount Joy | | | | Mount Misery | | | |
| | Height | Fenced | | Unfenced | | Fenced | | Unfenced | |
| Scientific Name | Class | Mean | SD | Mean | SD | Mean | SD | Mean | SD |
|---|---|---|---|---|---|---|---|---|---|
| *Acer platanoides* | 1 | 0.5 | 1.25 | | | | | | |
| | 3 | 0.1 | 0.26 | | | | | | |
| | 4 | 0.1 | 0.26 | | | | | | |
| *Acer rubrum* | 1 | 11.9 | 22.20 | 3.0 | 9.01 | 5.6 | 8.12 | 4.3 | 5.89 |
| | 2 | 0.6 | 1.24 | | | 0.3 | 0.90 | | |
| | 3 | 0.1 | 0.26 | | | 0.1 | 0.26 | | |
| *Ailanthus altissima* | 1 | 0.8 | 2.83 | | | | | | |
| *Carya glabra* | 1 | 0.1 | 0.35 | | | 0.1 | 0.26 | | |
| *Carya* spp. | 1 | | | 0.1 | 0.52 | | | | |
| *Cercis canadensis* | 1 | | | 0.1 | 0.26 | | | | |
| *Fraxinus americana* | 1 | 1.3 | 3.24 | 2.3 | 8.51 | 0.1 | 0.26 | | |
| | 2 | 0.1 | 0.35 | | | | | | |
| | 3 | 0.3 | 0.60 | | | | | | |
| | 4 | 0.1 | 0.52 | | | | | | |
| *Fraxinus* sp. | 1 | 0.5 | 1.60 | 0.9 | 2.50 | 0.1 | 0.26 | 0.5 | 1.55 |
| *Liriodendron tulipifera* | 1 | | | 0.3 | 1.05 | 0.1 | 0.26 | 0.2 | 0.77 |
| | 3 | 0.1 | 0.26 | | | | | | |
| | 4 | 0.1 | 0.26 | | | | | | |
| *Malus* spp. | 1 | 0.3 | 1.05 | | | | | | |
| | 2 | 0.1 | 0.26 | | | | | | |
| *Nyssa sylvatica* | 1 | 1.6 | 5.70 | 1.4 | 5.15 | 1.3 | 1.58 | 0.5 | 0.99 |
| | 2 | 0.2 | 0.56 | | | 0.7 | 1.58 | | |
| | 3 | 0.1 | 0.52 | | | 0.6 | 2.06 | | |
| | 4 | 0.1 | 0.26 | | | 0.1 | 0.35 | | |
| | 5 | 0.1 | 0.26 | | | 0.1 | 0.26 | | |
| | 6 | 0.1 | 0.26 | | | 0.1 | 0.52 | | |
| *Pinus strobus* | 1 | 1.07 | 1.28 | 0.1 | 0.35 | | | | |
| *Prunus avium* | 1 | 0.2 | 0.41 | | | | | | |
| *Prunus serotina* | 1 | 0.1 | 0.26 | | | 0.4 | 0.74 | 1.1 | 2.87 |
| | 2 | 0.1 | 0.26 | | | | | | |
| | 3 | 0.1 | 0.26 | | | 0.1 | 0.26 | | |
| *Quercus alba* | 1 | | | | | 0.2 | 0.77 | | |
| *Quercus coccinea* | 1 | | | | | | | 0.1 | 0.26 |
| *Quercus montana* | 1 | | | | | 9.5 | 22.35 | 0.1 | 0.26 |
| | 2 | 0.1 | 0.26 | | | 0.6 | 1.24 | | |
| *Quercus rubra* | 1 | 0.1 | 0.26 | | | 0.1 | 0.26 | 0.1 | 0.35 |
| | 2 | 0.1 | 0.26 | | | | | | |
| *Quercus* spp. | 1 | | | 0.1 | 0.26 | | | | |
| *Quercus velutina* | 1 | 0.2 | 0.41 | | | 0.6 | 1.12 | 0.1 | 0.26 |
| | 2 | | | | | 0.1 | 0.52 | | |
| *Sassafras albidum* | 1 | 3.1 | 6.06 | 1.4 | 4.10 | 4.0 | 3.96 | 2.4 | 4.21 |
| | 2 | | | | | 0.9 | 2.33 | | |
| | 3 | | | | | 0.2 | 0.41 | | |
| | 5 | | | | | 0.1 | 0.26 | | |
| *Ulmus rubra* | 2 | 0.1 | 0.26 | | | | | | |
| Unknown | 1 | | | | | | | 0.4 | 1.30 |

[a] Height classes: 1 = 0–25 cm, 2 = 26–50 cm, 3 = 51–75 cm, 4 = 76–100 cm, 5 = 101–125 cm, and 6 = 126–150 cm.

Table 8. Average number of tree seedlings per plot and standard deviation (SD), by height class, for Mount Joy and Mount Misery, Valley Forge National Historical Park, Pennsylvania, 2003.

| Height Class | Mount Joy | | | | Mount Misery | | | |
|---|---|---|---|---|---|---|---|---|
| | Fenced | | Unfenced | | Fenced | | Unfenced | |
| | Mean | SD | Mean | SD | Mean | SD | Mean | SD |
| 1 | 21.5 | 30.59 | 9.7 | 16.33 | 21.9 | 28.76 | 9.3 | 7.70 |
| 2 | 1.4 | 1.55 | | | 2.7 | 2.85 | | |
| 3 | 0.7 | 0.82 | | | 0.9 | 2.02 | | |
| 4 | 0.3 | 0.62 | | | 0.1 | 0.35 | | |
| 5 | 0.1 | 0.26 | | | 0.1 | 0.35 | | |
| 6 | 0.1 | 0.26 | | | 0.1 | 0.52 | | |

Principal Components Analysis

The first two eigenvectors of the principal components analysis explained 73% of the variation on Mount Misery and 70% of the variation on Mount Joy for the 2003 vegetation data (Table 9). The eigenvectors for Mount Misery indicated positive loadings on all four species types for the first eigenvector, and negative loadings on vines and herbs and positive loadings for trees and shrubs on the second eigenvector (Table 9). For Mount Joy, the first eigenvector loading was negative for trees and positive for all other species types, and the second eigenvector had a negative loading for herbs and positive loadings for the remaining species types (Table 9). Plots of the principal components scores for the first two eigenvectors indicated that fenced plots tended to have a greater number of plant species, as indicated by the greater scores for fenced plots (Figure 4).

Stocking Rates

Percent of plots adequately stocked (based on the criteria in Table 2), using all tree data, is presented in Table 10 for each year sampled. Excluding exotic tree species resulted in one less fenced plot in 1998 to be counted as adequately stocked. Excluding species not preferred by deer reduced 1998 and 2003 percentages by 3–4% for fenced plots (1 less plot classified as adequately stocked in each of the years). The mean number of weighted stem counts per plot increased in fenced plots and declined to zero in unfenced plots from 1993 to 2003 (Table 11).

Indicator Species

In 2003, four of six herbaceous species known to occur in the park that have been proposed as potential indicator species of the effects of deer browsing (Latham et al. 2005) occurred in nine of 30 fenced plots (1–3 species present), and one species (Jack-in-the-pulpit) was present in six of 30 unfenced plots. Whenever Jack-in-the-pulpit was present in an unfenced plot, it also occurred in the paired fenced plot (Table 12).

Table 9. Principal components eigenvectors using stem counts per plot for seedlings of tree species and number of times recorded per plot for shrub, vine, and herb species on Mount Misery and Mount Joy, Valley Forge National Historical Park, Pennsylvania, 2003.

| | Mount Misery | | Mount Joy | |
| Variable | Principal Component 1 | Principal Component 2 | Principal Component 1 | Principal Component 2 |
| --- | --- | --- | --- | --- |
| Vines | 0.6502 | -0.2727 | 0.4967 | 0.5970 |
| Herbs | 0.6609 | -0.2012 | 0.4893 | -0.3975 |
| Trees | 0.1498 | 0.7405 | -0.4233 | 0.6345 |
| Shrubs | 0.3435 | 0.5803 | 0.5785 | 0.2879 |
| Proportion of variation explained | 0.43 | 0.30 | 0.48 | 0.22 |

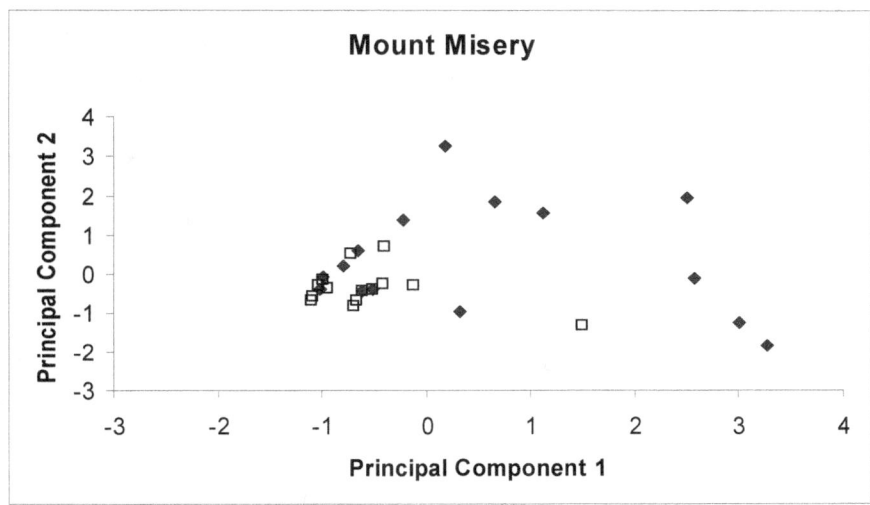

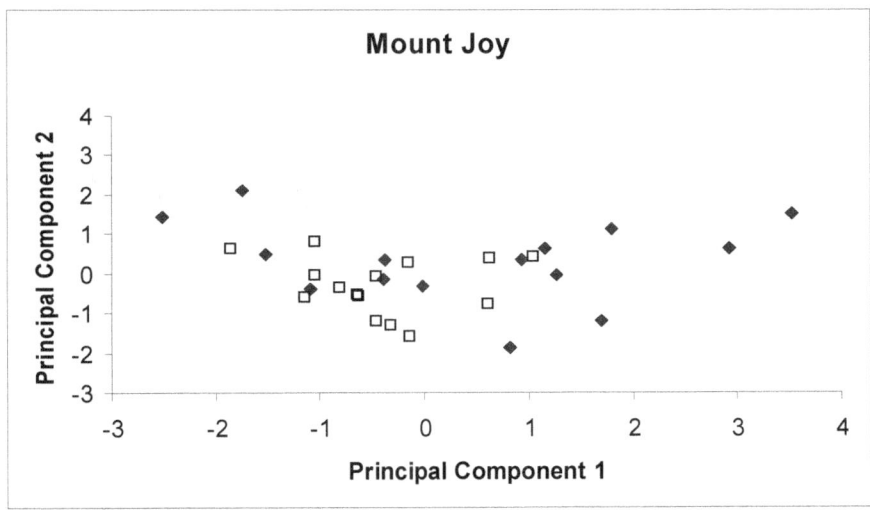

Figure 4. Plots of principal components scores for fenced (solid diamonds) and unfenced (open squares) plots on Mount Misery and Mount Joy, Valley Forge National Historical Park, Pennsylvania, 2003, using stem counts per plot for seedlings of tree species and number of times recorded per plot for shrub, vine, and herb species.

Table 10.  Percent of fenced and unfenced plots, using all tree data, on both Mount Misery and Mount Joy adequately stocked (*n* = 30 for each cell), Valley Forge National Historical Park, Pennsylvania, 1993–2003.

| Plot Type | 1993 | 1995 | 1998 | 2003 |
|-----------|------|------|------|------|
| Fenced    | 3    | 3    | 13   | 27   |
| Unfenced  | 3    | 0    | 0    | 0    |

Table 11.  Mean number of stems (weighted counts) per fenced and unfenced plot on both Mount Misery and Mount Joy, Valley Forge National Historical Park, Pennsylvania, 1993–2003.

| Plot Type | 1993 | | 1995 | | 1998 | | 2003 | |
|-----------|------|------|------|------|------|------|------|------|
|           | $\bar{x}$ | SE | $\bar{x}$ | SE | $\bar{x}$ | SE | $\bar{x}$ | SE |
| Fenced    | 4.8  | 2.6  | 4.4  | 1.2  | 7.5  | 2.2  | 25.2 | 8.9  |
| Unfenced  | 1.4  | 0.9  | 0.2  | 0.1  | 0.1  | 0.1  | 0.0  |      |

Table 12.  Occurrence (0 = absent; 1 = present) of Jack-in-the-pulpit (*Arisaema triphyllum*), wild sarsaparilla (*Aralia nudicaulis*), sweet cicely (*Osmorhiza claytoni*), Indian cucumber root (*Medeola virginiana*), and *Trillium* spp. in fenced and unfenced plots on Mount Misery and Mount Joy, Valley Forge National Historical Park, Pennsylvania, 1993–2003.

| Area and Site Number | Treatment | Species | 1993 | 1995 | 1998 | 2003 |
|---|---|---|---|---|---|---|
| Mount Misery | | | | | | |
| 7 | Fenced | *Medeola virginiana* | 1 | 1 | 1 | 0 |
| 7 | Unfenced | *Medeola virginiana* | 1 | 0 | 0 | 0 |
| 8 | Fenced | *Aralia nudicaulis* | 0 | 0 | 1 | 1 |
| 8 | Unfenced | *Aralia nudicaulis* | 0 | 0 | 0 | 0 |
| 9 | Fenced | *Aralia nudicaulis* | 0 | 0 | 1 | 0 |
| 9 | Unfenced | *Aralia nudicaulis* | 0 | 0 | 0 | 0 |
| 10 | Fenced | *Medeola virginiana* | 0 | 0 | 0 | 0 |
| 10 | Unfenced | *Medeola virginiana* | 1 | 0 | 1 | 0 |
| 11 | Fenced | *Aralia nudicaulis* | 1 | 0 | 1 | 1 |
| 11 | Unfenced | *Aralia nudicaulis* | 0 | 0 | 0 | 0 |
| 11 | Fenced | *Arisaema triphyllum* | 0 | 0 | 0 | 1 |
| 11 | Unfenced | *Arisaema triphyllum* | 0 | 0 | 0 | 1 |
| 11 | Fenced | *Medeola virginiana* | 0 | 1 | 1 | 1 |
| 11 | Unfenced | *Medeola virginiana* | 1 | 1 | 1 | 0 |
| 11 | Fenced | *Trillium* spp. | 0 | 1 | 0 | 0 |
| 11 | Unfenced | *Trillium* spp. | 1 | 0 | 0 | 0 |
| Mount Joy | | | | | | |
| 16 | Fenced | *Arisaema triphyllum* | 0 | 1 | 1 | 1 |
| 16 | Unfenced | *Arisaema triphyllum* | 0 | 1 | 0 | 1 |
| 17 | Fenced | *Arisaema triphyllum* | 0 | 0 | 1 | 1 |
| 17 | Unfenced | *Arisaema triphyllum* | 0 | 0 | 1 | 1 |
| 17 | Fenced | *Osmorhiza claytoni* | 0 | 0 | 1 | 1 |
| 17 | Unfenced | *Osmorhiza claytoni* | 0 | 0 | 0 | 0 |
| 17 | Fenced | *Trillium* spp. | 1 | 0 | 0 | 0 |
| 17 | Unfenced | *Trillium* spp. | 1 | 0 | 0 | 0 |
| 19 | Fenced | *Arisaema triphyllum* | 0 | 0 | 0 | 1 |
| 19 | Unfenced | *Arisaema triphyllum* | 0 | 0 | 1 | 1 |
| 19 | Fenced | *Osmorhiza claytoni* | 0 | 0 | 1 | 0 |
| 19 | Unfenced | *Osmorhiza claytoni* | 0 | 0 | 0 | 0 |
| 21 | Fenced | *Aralia nudicaulis* | 0 | 0 | 1 | 0 |
| 21 | Unfenced | *Aralia nudicaulis* | 0 | 0 | 0 | 0 |
| 21 | Fenced | *Osmorhiza claytoni* | 1 | 1 | 0 | 0 |
| 21 | Unfenced | *Osmorhiza claytoni* | 0 | 0 | 0 | 0 |
| 24 | Fenced | *Arisaema triphyllum* | 0 | 0 | 0 | 1 |
| 24 | Unfenced | *Arisaema triphyllum* | 0 | 0 | 0 | 0 |
| 25 | Fenced | *Arisaema triphyllum* | 0 | 1 | 0 | 1 |
| 25 | Unfenced | *Arisaema triphyllum* | 0 | 1 | 0 | 1 |
| 25 | Fenced | *Osmorhiza claytoni* | 1 | 1 | 0 | 0 |
| 25 | Unfenced | *Osmorhiza claytoni* | 0 | 0 | 0 | 0 |
| 25 | Fenced | *Trillium* spp. | 1 | 0 | 0 | 0 |
| 25 | Unfenced | *Trillium* spp. | 0 | 0 | 0 | 0 |
| 27 | Fenced | *Medeola virginiana* | 0 | 0 | 0 | 0 |
| 27 | Unfenced | *Medeola virginiana* | 0 | 1 | 0 | 0 |
| 28 | Fenced | *Arisaema triphyllum* | 0 | 1 | 0 | 1 |
| 28 | Unfenced | *Arisaema triphyllum* | 0 | 1 | 1 | 1 |
| 28 | Fenced | *Osmorhiza claytoni* | 0 | 0 | 0 | 0 |
| 28 | Unfenced | *Osmorhiza claytoni* | 0 | 1 | 0 | 0 |
| 29 | Fenced | *Arisaema triphyllum* | 0 | 1 | 0 | 1 |
| 29 | Unfenced | *Arisaema triphyllum* | 0 | 1 | 0 | 0 |

# Conclusions

The statistical analysis of species richness indicates substantial changes between 1993 and 2003, during which richness generally increased over time in fenced plots and and exhibited no change or a slight decline in unfenced plots. Species richness in fenced plots and in unfenced plots was greater on Mount Joy than on Mount Misery in each year sampled. The occurrence of specific species in fenced and unfenced plots over time, and in the two forest stands, can be studied in Appendixes B–E. Mean stem density of tree seedlings in fenced plots increased over time, but because of high variability among plots we failed to detect a statistically significant change. In 2003, unfenced plots generally contained about one-third the number of tree seedlings present in fenced plots.

Advanced regeneration stocking rates are a measure developed by foresters (McWilliams et al. 2002) to assess the potential for forests to regenerate following timber harvest. By applying this metric to fenced and unfenced plots, it indicates that the percentage of fenced plots which have sufficient advanced regeneration has increased (from 3% to 27% of plots; Table 5) during 1993–2003; whereas since 1995 no unfenced plots have had adequate advanced regeneration. Table 7 provides a means to examine species-specific changes. Finally, neither fenced nor unfenced plots generally contained a large number of exotic species (Table 5).

The principal components analysis and resulting plots of the first two eigenvectors (Figure 4) are another way to visualize the differences between fenced and unfenced plots. Most unfenced plots are clustered together because they are similar in number of species by plant type (herbaceous, vine, tree, or shrub), whereas the fenced plots have been released from deer browsing and differences among plots are expressed by a greater scatter of points in Figure 4. However, fenced plots still exhibit substantial overlap with unfenced plots.

A number of herbaceous species have been identified as potential indicator species regarding the effects of deer browsing (Latham et al. 2005). The indicator species that occur in Valley Forge National Historical Park (Jack-in-the-pulpit, wild sarsaparilla, sweet cicely, Indian cucumber root, *Trillium* spp., and white wood aster) are relatively rare. In 2003, four of these species were found in only nine of 30 paired sites, of which six sites contained just one species (Jack-in-the-pulpit) in the unfenced plot. More plots, perhaps each plot larger in size, or a longer monitoring time will likely be needed to detect changes with these indicator species.

# Literature Cited

Braun, E. L. 1950. Deciduous Forests of Eastern North America. Blackburn Press. Caldwell, NJ. 576 pp.

Davis, C., J. Comiskey, K. Callahan. 2006. MidAtlantic Park Profiles. Appendix 2. National Park Service. Mid-Atlantic Inventory & Monitoring Network. www.nature.nps.gov/im/units/midn/Phase_1_Report/Appendix_2._Park_Profiles.pdf.

Kasmer, J., P. Kasmer, and S. Ware. 1984. Edaphic factors and vegetation in the Piedmont Lowland of southeastern Pennsylvania. Castanea 49:147–157.

Keys, J. E., Jr., C. A. Carpenter, S. L. Hooks, F. G. Koenig, W. H. McNab, W. E. Russell, M. Smith. 1995. Ecological Units of the Eastern United States, First Approximation. 1:3,500,000 map and accompanying map unit tables. USDA Forest Service.

Latham, R. E., J. Beyea, J. M. Benner, C. Adams Dunn, M. A. Fajvan, R. R. Freed, M. Grund, S. B. Horsley, A. F. Rhoads, and B. P. Shissler. 2005. Managing white-tailed deer from an ecosystem perspective: Pennsylvania case study. Report by the Deer Management Forum for Audubon Pennsylvania and Pennsylvania Habitat Alliance. Harrisburg, PA.

McWilliams, W. H., T. W. Bowersox, P. H. Brose, D. A. Devlin, J. C. Finley, K. W. Gottschalk, S. Horsley, S. L. King, B. M. LaPoint, T. W. Lister, L. H. McCormick, G. W. Miller, C. T. Scott, H. Steele, K. C. Steiner, S. L. Stout, J. A. Westfall, and R. L. White. 2002. Measuring tree seedlings and associated understory vegetation in Pennsylvania's forests. Page 21–26 in Proceedings of the Fourth Annual Forest Inventory and Analysis Symposium. McRoberts, R. E., Reams, G. A., Van Deusen, P. C., McWilliams, W. H., and Cieszewski, C, J., editors. General Technical Report NC-252. U.S. Department of Agriculture, Forest Service, North Central Research Station. St. Paul, MN.

Pennsylvania Geological Survey. 1981. Map 61, 591: Valley Forge Quadrangle. Atlas of Preliminary Geologic Quadrangle Maps of Pennsylvania. Pennsylvania Geological Survey.

Pennsylvania Bureau of Topographic and Geographic Survey. 2001. Bedrock Geology of Pennsylvania: shape-file format, Reading 30'×60' quadrangle. Pennsylvania Bureau of Topographic and Geographic Survey, DCNR.

Pennsuylvania Department of Conservation and Natural Resources. 2005. Invasive Exotic Plant Managment Tutorial for Natural Lands Managers. Mid-Atlantic Exotic Pest Plant Council, Inc. Lisa Smith, Principal Investigator. http://www.dcnr.state.pa.us/forestry/invasivetutorial/List.htm.

Podniesinski. G. S., L. A. Sneddon, J. Lundgren, H. Devine, B. Slocumb, and F. Koch. 2005. Vegetation classification and mapping of Valley Forge National Historical Park. Technical Report NPS/NER/NRTR—2005/028. National Park Service. Philadelphia, PA.

Rhoads, A. F. and Klein, Jr. 1993. The vascular flora of Pennsylvania: annotated checklist and atlas. American Philosophical Society. Philadelphia, PA.

Rhoads, A. F., D. Ryan, and E. W. Aderman. 1989. Land use study of Valley Forge National Historical Park. Final Report. U.S. Department of Interior, National Park Service, Valley Forge National Historical Park. Contract #: CA4000-7-8021.

SAS Institute, Inc. 2003. SAS version 9.1 for Windows. Cary, NC.

Storm, G. L., and A. S. Ross. 1992. Draft. Manual for monitoring vegetation on public lands in mid-Atlantic United States. Pennsylvania Cooperative Fish and Wildlife Research Unit. University Park, PA. 89 pp.

United States Department of Agriculture Soil Conservation Service (USDA SCS). 1967. Soil Survey Montgomery County Pennsylvania. The Pennsylvania State University and Pennsylvania Department of Agriculture.

Appendix A. Tree species observed in vegetation plots, and their deer preference, on Mount Misery and Mount Joy, Valley Forge National Historical Park, Pennsylvania, 1993–2003.

| Species | Deer Preference[a] | Notes |
|---|---|---|
| tree of heaven | 0 | Exotic |
| Norway maple | 1 | Exotic, assumed to be preferred like all native *Acer* |
| princess tree | 0 | Exotic |
| red maple | 1 | |
| silver maple | 1 | |
| sugar maple | 1 | |
| black birch | 1 | |
| hornbeam | 0 | Unknown preference |
| pignut hickory | 0 | |
| American chestnut | 1 | Unknown preference |
| hackberry | 0 | |
| redbud | 0 | Unknown preference |
| flowering dogwood | 1 | |
| American beech | 0 | |
| white ash | 1 | |
| yellow poplar | 1 | Highly preferred |
| crabapple | 1 | |
| black gum | 1 | Highly preferred |
| hop hornbeam | 0 | |
| white pine | 0 | |
| sweet cherry | 0 | |
| black cherry | 0 | |
| white oak | 1 | |
| scarlet oak | 1 | Highly preferred |
| chestnut oak | 1 | Highly preferred |
| northern red oak | 1 | Highly preferred |
| black oak | 1 | Highly preferred |
| sassafrass | 1 | |
| American elm | 0 | |
| slippery (red) elm | 0 | |

[a] 0 - Species ranked as having low or unknown preference by deer.
 1 - Species ranked as having moderate or high preference by deer.

Rankings from Latham et al. (2005).

Appendix B. The year species were observed during sampling of unfenced plots on Mount Misery, Valley Forge National Historical Park, Pennsylvania, 1993–2003.

| Scientific name | Common name | Plant type | Exotic[a] | Invasive[b] | 1993 | 1995 | 1998 | 2003 |
|---|---|---|---|---|---|---|---|---|
| Arisaema triphyllum | Jack-in-the-pulpit | Herb | No | No | | | | X |
| Chimaphila maculata | striped wintergreen | Herb | No | No | | | | X |
| Dennstaedtia punctilobula | hay scented fern | Herb | No | No | | | | X |
| Fraxinus sp. | ash | Tree | No | No | | | | X |
| Monotropa uniflora | Indian-pipe | Herb | No | No | | | | X |
| Quercus coccinea | scarlet oak | Tree | No | No | | | | X |
| Quercus velutina | black oak | Tree | No | No | | | | X |
| Amelanchier sp. | juneberry | Herb | No | No | | | X | |
| Berberis thunbergii | Japanese barberry | Shrub | Yes | Yes | | | X | |
| Carya ovata | shagbark hickory | Tree | No | No | | | X | |
| Celastrus orbiculatus | oriental bittersweet | Vine | Yes | Yes | | | X | |
| Cornus florida | flowering dogwood | Tree | No | No | | | X | |
| Pteridium aquilinum | bracken fern | Herb | No | No | | | X | |
| Rhododendron periclymenoides | pink azalea | Shrub | No | No | | | X | |
| Rubus occidentalis | black raspberry | Herb | No | No | | | X | |
| Carex digitalis | sedge | Herb | No | No | | | X | X |
| Gaylussacia baccata | black huckleberry | Shrub | No | No | | | X | X |
| Maianthemum canadense | wild lily of the valley | Herb | No | No | | | X | X |
| Betula lenta | black birch | Tree | No | No | | X | | |
| Castanea dentata | American chestnut | Tree | No | No | | X | | |
| Ostrya virginiana | hop hornbeam | Tree | No | No | | X | | |
| Prunus serotina | wild black cherry | Tree | No | No | | X | X | X |
| Thelypteris noveboracensis | New York fern | Herb | No | No | | X | X | X |
| Carpinus caroliniana | hornbeam | Tree | No | No | X | | | |
| Maianthemum racemosum | false Solomon's seal | Herb | No | No | X | | | |
| Panax quinquefolius | ginseng | Herb | No | No | X | | | |
| Polygonatum sp. | Solomon's seal | Herb | No | No | X | | | |
| Symplocarpus foetidus | skunk cabbage | Herb | No | No | X | | | |
| Trillium sp. | trillium | Herb | No | No | X | | | |
| Toxicodendron radicans | poison ivy | Vine | No | No | X | | X | |

| Scientific name | Common name | Plant type | Exotic[a] | Invasive[b] | 1993 | 1995 | 1998 | 2003 |
|---|---|---|---|---|---|---|---|---|
| *Fagus grandifolia* | American beech | Tree | No | No | X | X | | |
| *Microstegium vimineum* | stilt grass | Herb | Yes | Yes | X | X | | |
| *Phlox* sp. | phlox | Herb | No | No | X | X | | |
| *Quercus alba* | white oak | Tree | No | No | X | X | | |
| *Smilax rotundifolia* | greenbrier | Vine | No | No | X | X | | |
| *Kalmia latifolia* | mountain laurel | Shrub | No | No | X | X | | X |
| *Quercus rubra* | northern red oak | Tree | No | No | X | X | | X |
| *Athyrium filix-femina* | northern lady fern | Herb | No | No | X | X | X | |
| *Chimaphila umbellata* | pipsissewa | Herb | No | No | X | X | X | |
| *Medeola virginiana* | Indian cucumber root | Herb | No | No | X | X | X | |
| *Viburnum acerifolium* | maple-leaf viburnum | Shrub | No | No | X | X | X | |
| *Acer rubrum* | red maple | Tree | No | No | X | X | X | X |
| *Hamamelis virginiana* | witch hazel | Shrub | No | No | X | X | X | X |
| *Liriodendron tulipifera* | tuliptree | Tree | No | No | X | X | X | X |
| *Nyssa sylvatica* | blackgum | Tree | No | No | X | X | X | X |
| *Parthenocissus quinquefolia* | Virginia creeper | Vine | No | No | X | X | X | X |
| *Quercus montana* | chestnut oak | Tree | No | No | X | X | X | X |
| *Sassafras albidum* | sassafras | Tree | No | No | X | X | X | X |
| *Vaccinium corymbosum* | highbush blueberry | Shrub | No | No | X | X | X | X |

[a] Rhoads, A. F., and W. M. Klein, Jr. 1993. The Vascular Flora of Pennsylvania: Annotated Checklist and Atlas. American Philosophical Society. Philadelphia, PA.

[b] Invasive: Pennsuylvania Department of Conservation and Natural Resources. 2005. Invasive Exotic Plant Managment Tutorial for Natural Lands Managers. Mid-Atlantic Exotic Pest Plant Council, Inc. Lisa Smith, Principal Investigator. http://www.dcnr.state.pa.us/forestry/invasivetutorial/List.htm.

Appendix C. The year species were observed during sampling of fenced plots on Mount Misery, Valley Forge National Historical Park, Pennsylvania, 1993–2003.

| Scientific name | Common name | Plant type | Exotic[a] | Invasive[b] | 1993 | 1995 | 1998 | 2003 |
|---|---|---|---|---|---|---|---|---|
| Arisaema triphyllum | Jack-in-the-pulpit | Herb | No | No | | | | X |
| Chimaphila maculata | striped wintergreen | Herb | No | No | | | | X |
| Fraxinus americana | white ash | Tree | No | No | | | | X |
| Fraxinus sp. | ash | Tree | No | No | | | | X |
| Gaylussacia frondosa | blue huckleberry | Shrub | No | No | | | | X |
| Gaylussacia sp. | huckleberry species | Shrub | No | No | | | | X |
| Isotria verticillata | whorled pogonia | Herb | No | No | | | | X |
| Polygonum caespitosum | smartweed | Herb | Yes | No | | | | X |
| Pteridium aquilinum | bracken fern | Herb | No | No | | | | X |
| Quercus velutina | black oak | Tree | No | No | | | | X |
| Rubus pensilvanicus | Pennsylvania blackberry | Herb | No | No | | | | X |
| Carpinus caroliniana | hornbeam | Tree | No | No | | | X | |
| Lysimachia quadrifolia | whorled loosestrife | Herb | No | No | | | X | |
| Prenanthes altissima | rattlesnake root | Herb | No | No | | | X | |
| Prunus avium | sweet cherry | Tree | Yes | No | | | X | |
| Rubus pubescens | dwarf raspberry | Herb | No | No | | | X | |
| Toxicodendron radicans | poison ivy | Vine | No | No | | | X | |
| Dennstaedtia punctilobula | hay scented fern | Herb | No | No | | | X | X |
| Desmodium nudiflorum | naked tick-trefoil | Herb | No | No | | | X | X |
| Gaylussacia baccata | black huckleberry | Shrub | No | No | | | X | X |
| Kalmia angustifolia | sheep laurel | Herb | No | No | | | X | X |
| Polygonatum biflorum | smooth Solomon's seal | Herb | No | No | | | X | X |
| Prunus serotina | wild black cherry | Tree | No | No | | | X | X |
| Rhododendron periclymenoides | pink azalea | Shrub | No | No | | | X | X |
| Viburnum dentatum | arrowwood vibernum | Shrub | No | No | | | X | X |
| Boehmeria cylindrica | false nettle | Herb | No | No | | X | | |
| Lactuca canadensis | wild lettuce | Herb | No | No | | X | | |
| Rubus recurvicaulis | dewberry | Herb | No | No | | X | | |

| Scientific name | Common name | Plant type | Exotic[a] | Invasive[b] | 1993 | 1995 | 1998 | 2003 |
|---|---|---|---|---|---|---|---|---|
| *Trillium* sp. | trillium | Herb | No | No | | X | | |
| *Viola* sp. | violet | Herb | No | No | | X | | |
| *Acer saccharinum* | silver maple | Tree | No | No | | X | X | |
| *Carya glabra* | pignut hickory | Tree | No | No | | X | X | X |
| *Thelypteris noveboracensis* | New York fern | Herb | No | No | | X | X | X |
| *Uvularia perfoliata* | bellwort | Herb | No | No | | X | X | X |
| *Vitis aestivalis* | summer grape | Vine | No | No | | X | X | X |
| *Lonicera japonica* | Japanese honeysuckle | Vine | Yes | Yes | X | | | |
| *Microstegium vimineum* | stilt grass | Herb | Yes | Yes | X | | | |
| *Pilea pumila* | clearweed | Herb | No | No | X | | | |
| *Polygonum aviculare* | knotweed | Herb | Yes | No | X | | X | |
| *Aralia nudicaulis* | wild sarsparilla | Herb | No | No | X | | X | X |
| *Amphicarpa bracteata* | hog peanut | Herb | No | No | X | X | | |
| *Celastrus orbiculatus* | Oriental bittersweet | Vine | Yes | Yes | X | X | | |
| *Fagus grandifolia* | American beech | Tree | No | No | X | X | | |
| *Panax quinquefolius* | ginseng | Herb | No | No | X | X | | |
| *Phlox* sp. | phlox | Herb | No | No | X | X | | |
| *Athyrium filix-femina* | northern lady fern | Herb | No | No | X | X | X | |
| *Chimaphila umbellata* | pipsissewa | Herb | No | No | X | X | X | |
| *Cornus florida* | flowering dogwood | Tree | No | No | X | X | X | |
| *Acer rubrum* | red maple | Tree | No | No | X | X | X | X |
| *Carex communis* | sedge | Herb | No | No | X | X | X | X |
| *Hamamelis virginiana* | witch hazel | Shrub | No | No | X | X | X | X |
| *Kalmia latifolia* | mountain laurel | Shrub | No | No | X | X | X | X |
| *Liriodendron tulipifera* | tuliptree | Tree | No | No | X | X | X | X |
| *Maianthemum racemosum* | false Solomon's seal | Herb | No | No | X | X | X | X |
| *Medeola virginiana* | Indian cucumber root | Herb | No | No | X | X | X | X |
| *Nyssa sylvatica* | blackgum | Tree | No | No | X | X | X | X |
| *Parthenocissus quinquefolia* | Virginia creeper | Vine | No | No | X | X | X | X |
| *Quercus alba* | white oak | Tree | No | No | X | X | X | X |
| *Quercus montana* | chestnut oak | Tree | No | No | X | X | X | X |

| Scientific name | Common name | Plant type | Exotic[a] | Invasive[b] | 1993 | 1995 | 1998 | 2003 |
|---|---|---|---|---|---|---|---|---|
| *Quercus rubra* | northern red oak | Tree | No | No | X | X | X | X |
| *Sassafras albidum* | sassafras | Tree | No | No | X | X | X | X |
| *Smilax glauca* | greenbrier | Vine | No | No | X | X | X | X |
| *Symphyotrichum divaricatum* | white wood aster | Herb | No | No | X | X | X | X |
| *Vaccinium angustifolium* | lowbush blueberry | Shrub | No | No | X | X | X | X |
| *Viburnum acerifolium* | maple-leaf viburnum | Shrub | No | No | X | X | X | X |

[a] Rhoads, A. F., and W. M. Klein, Jr. 1993. The Vascular Flora of Pennsylvania: Annotated Checklist and Atlas. American Philosophical Society. Philadelphia, PA.

[b] Invasive: Pennsuylvania Department of Conservation and Natural Resources. 2005. Invasive Exotic Plant Managment Tutorial for Natural Lands Managers. Mid-Atlantic Exotic Pest Plant Council, Inc. Lisa Smith, Principal Investigator. http://www.dcnr.state.pa.us/forestry/invasivetutorial/List.htm.

Appendix D. The year species were observed during sampling of unfenced plots on Mount Joy, Valley Forge National Historical Park, Pennsylvania, 1993–2003.

| Scientific name | Common name | Plant type | Exotic[a] | Invasive[b] | 1993 | 1995 | 1998 | 2003 |
|---|---|---|---|---|---|---|---|---|
| Euonymus alata | burning bush | Shrub | Yes | Yes | | | | X |
| Fraxinus sp. | ash | Tree | No | No | | | | X |
| Ligustrum vulgare | common privet | Shrub | Yes | Yes | | | | X |
| Lonicera maackii | amur honeysuckle | Shrub | Yes | Yes | | | | X |
| Quercus sp. | oak species | Tree | No | No | | | | X |
| Ranunculus bulbosus | bulbous buttercup | Herb | Yes | No | | | | X |
| Rubus pensilvanicus | Pennsylvania blackberry | Herb | No | No | | | | X |
| Taraxacum officinale | common dandelion | Herb | Yes | No | | | | X |
| Vitis sp. | grape | Vine | No | No | | | | X |
| Ageratina altissima | white snakeroot | Herb | No | No | | | X | |
| Cornus florida | flowering dogwood | Tree | No | No | | | X | |
| Sanicula marilandica | black snake root | Herb | No | No | | | X | |
| Cercis canadensis | redbud | Tree | No | No | | | X | X |
| Fraxinus americana | white ash | Tree | No | No | | | X | X |
| Pinus strobus | white pine | Tree | No | No | | | X | X |
| Viburnum prunifolium | black haw | Shrub | No | No | | | X | X |
| Vitis aestivalis | summer grape | Vine | No | No | | | X | X |
| Vitis vulpina | frost grape | Vine | No | No | | | X | X |
| Acer platanoides | norway maple | Tree | Yes | Yes | | X | | |
| Leersia virginica | white grass | Herb | No | No | | X | | |
| Medeola virginiana | Indian cucumber root | Herb | No | No | | X | | |
| Osmorhiza claytoni | sweet cicely | Herb | No | No | | X | | |
| Ulmus rubra | slippery elm | Tree | No | No | | X | | |
| Arisaema triphyllum | Jack-in-the-pulpit | Herb | No | No | | X | X | X |
| Polygonum aviculare | knotweed | Herb | Yes | No | | X | X | X |
| Viola sp. | violet | Herb | No | No | | X | X | X |
| Lycopus sp. | water-horehound | Herb | No | No | X | | | |
| Maianthemum racemosum | false Solomon's seal | Herb | No | No | X | | | |
| Prunus avium | sweet cherry | Tree | Yes | No | X | | | |
| Ranunculus recurvatus | hooked crowfoot | Herb | No | No | X | | | |
| Rubus hispidus | swamp dewberry | Herb | No | No | X | | | |

| Scientific name | Common name | Plant type | Exotic[a] | Invasive[b] | 1993 | 1995 | 1998 | 2003 |
|---|---|---|---|---|---|---|---|---|
| Trillium sp. | trillium | Herb | No | No | X | | | |
| Uvularia perfoliata | bellwort | Herb | No | No | X | | | |
| Carya sp. | hickory | Tree | No | No | X | | | X |
| Polygonatum sp. | Solomon's seal | Herb | No | No | X | | | X |
| Smilax sp. | greenbriar | Vine | No | No | X | | | X |
| Viburnum acerifolium | maple-leaf viburnum | Shrub | No | No | X | | | X |
| Prunus serotina | wild black cherry | Tree | No | No | X | | X | |
| Circaea alpina | enchanter's nightshade | Herb | No | No | X | | X | X |
| Liriodendron tulipifera | tuliptree | Tree | No | No | X | | X | X |
| Toxicodendron radicans | poison ivy | Vine | No | No | X | | X | X |
| Fagus grandifolia | American beech | Tree | No | No | X | X | | |
| Fragaria virginiana | wild strawberry | Herb | No | No | X | X | | |
| Galium circaezans | wild licorice | Herb | No | No | X | X | | |
| Malva neglecta | common mallow | Herb | Yes | No | X | X | | |
| Pastinaca sativa | wild parsnip | Herb | Yes | No | X | X | | |
| Phlox sp. | phlox | Herb | No | No | X | X | | |
| Polygonum virginianum | jumpseed | Herb | No | No | X | X | | |
| Prunus virginiana | choke cherry | Tree | No | No | X | X | | |
| Quercus montana | chestnut oak | Tree | No | No | X | X | | |
| Quercus rubra | northern red oak | Tree | No | No | X | X | | |
| Symphyotrichum divaricatum | white wood aster | Herb | No | No | X | X | | |
| Carex pensylvanica | sedge | Herb | No | No | X | X | | X |
| Carex sp. | sedge | Herb | No | No | X | X | | X |
| Carex swanii | sedge | Herb | No | No | X | X | | X |
| Betula lenta | black birch | Tree | No | No | X | X | X | |
| Acer rubrum | red maple | Tree | No | No | X | X | X | X |
| Alliaria petiolata | garlic-mustard | Herb | Yes | Yes | X | X | X | X |
| Cardamine impatiens | bitter-cress | Herb | Yes | No | X | X | X | X |
| Celastrus orbiculatus | Oriental bittersweet | Vine | Yes | Yes | X | X | X | X |
| Duchesnea indica | Indian strawberry | Herb | Yes | No | X | X | X | X |
| Lindera benzoin | spicebush | Shrub | No | No | X | X | X | X |
| Lonicera japonica | Japanese honeysuckle | Vine | Yes | Yes | X | X | X | X |
| Microstegium vimineum | stilt grass | Herb | Yes | Yes | X | X | X | X |
| Nyssa sylvatica | blackgum | Tree | No | No | X | X | X | X |

| Scientific name | Common name | Plant type | Exotic[a] | Invasive[b] | 1993 | 1995 | 1998 | 2003 |
|---|---|---|---|---|---|---|---|---|
| *Oxalis stricta* | common yellow wood-sorrel | Herb | No | No | X | X | X | X |
| *Parthenocissus quinquefolia* | Virginia creeper | Herb | No | No | X | X | X | X |
| *Pilea pumila* | clearweed | Herb | No | No | X | X | X | X |
| *Polygonum caespitosum* | smartweed | Herb | Yes | No | X | X | X | X |
| *Rubus phoenicolasius* | wineberry | Herb | Yes | Yes | X | X | X | X |
| *Sassafras albidum* | sassafras | Tree | No | No | X | X | X | X |
| *Vaccinium pallidum* | blueberry | Shrub | No | No | X | X | X | X |
| *Vaccinium* sp. | blueberry | Shrub | No | No | X | X | X | X |
| *Vaccinium stamineum* | deerberry | Shrub | No | No | X | X | X | X |

[a] Rhoads, A. F., and W. M. Klein, Jr. 1993. The Vascular Flora of Pennsylvania: Annotated Checklist and Atlas. American Philosophical Society. Philadelphia, PA.

[b] Invasive: Pennsuylvania Department of Conservation and Natural Resources. 2005. Invasive Exotic Plant Managment Tutorial for Natural Lands Managers. Mid-Atlantic Exotic Pest Plant Council, Inc. Lisa Smith, Principal Investigator. http://www.dcnr.state.pa.us/forestry/invasivetutorial/List.htm.

Appendix E: The year species were observed during sampling of fenced plots on Mount Joy, Valley Forge National Historical Park, Pennsylvania, 1993–2003.

| Scientific name | Common name | Plant type | Exotic[a] | Invasive[b] | 1993 | 1995 | 1998 | 2003 |
|---|---|---|---|---|---|---|---|---|
| *Ageratina altissima* | white snakeroot | Herb | No | No | | | | X |
| *Ailanthus altissima* | tree of heaven | Tree | Yes | Yes | | | | X |
| *Chimaphila maculata* | striped wintergreen | Herb | No | No | | | | X |
| *Desmodium nudiflorum* | naked tick-trefoil | Herb | No | No | | | | X |
| *Dryopteris carthusiana* | spinulose woodfern | Herb | No | No | | | | X |
| *Dryopteris marginalis* | marginal woodfern | Herb | No | No | | | | X |
| *Euonymus alata* | burning bush | Shrub | Yes | Yes | | | | X |
| *Fraxinus* sp. | ash | Tree | No | No | | | | X |
| *Geum canadense* | white avens | Herb | No | No | | | | X |
| *Malus* sp. | crabapple | Tree | No | No | | | | X |
| *Monotropa uniflora* | Indian-pipe | Herb | No | No | | | | X |
| *Phytolacca americana* | pokeweed | Herb | No | No | | | | X |
| *Quercus velutina* | black oak | Tree | No | No | | | | X |
| *Sanicula* sp. | sanicle | Herb | No | No | | | | X |
| *Smilax* sp. | greenbriar | Vine | No | No | | | | X |
| *Vitis* sp. | grape | Vine | No | No | | | | X |
| *Acer saccharum* | sugar maple | Tree | No | No | | | X | |
| *Aralia nudicaulis* | wild sarsaparilla | Herb | No | No | | | X | |
| *Chimaphila umbellata* | pipsissewa | Herb | No | No | | | X | |
| *Lysimachia quadrifolia* | whorled loosestrife | Herb | No | No | | | X | |
| *Phryma leptostachya* | lopseed | Herb | No | No | | | X | |
| *Polygonum aviculare* | knotweed | Herb | Yes | No | | | X | |
| *Rubus pubescens* | dwarf raspberry | Herb | No | No | | | X | |
| *Ulmus americana* | American elm | Tree | No | No | | | X | |
| *Uvularia sessilifolia* | wild oats | Herb | No | No | | | X | |
| *Cimicifuga racemosa* | black cohosh | Herb | No | No | | | X | X |
| *Eupatorium* sp. | joe pye weed | Herb | No | No | | | X | X |
| *Eupatorium purpureum* | sweetscented joe pye weed | Herb | No | No | | | X | X |
| *Lonicera maackii* | amur honeysuckle | Shrub | Yes | Yes | | | X | X |
| *Lonicera morrowii* | morrow honeysuckle | Shrub | Yes | Yes | | | X | X |
| *Prunus serotina* | wild black cherry | Tree | No | No | | | X | X |
| *Pteridium aquilinum* | bracken fern | Herb | No | No | | | X | X |

| Scientific name | Common name | Plant type | Exotic[a] | Invasive[b] | 1993 | 1995 | 1998 | 2003 |
|---|---|---|---|---|---|---|---|---|
| *Rhododendron periclymenoides* | pink azalea | Shrub | No | No | | | X | X |
| *Rubus pensilvanicus* | Pennsylvania blackberry | Herb | No | No | | | X | X |
| *Vitis vulpina* | frost grape | Vine | No | No | | | X | X |
| *Acer saccharinum* | silver maple | Tree | No | No | | X | | |
| *Celtis occidentalis* | hackberry | Tree | No | No | | X | | |
| *Fragaria virginiana* | wild strawberry | Herb | No | No | | X | | |
| *Hamamelis virginiana* | witch hazel | Shrub | No | No | | X | | |
| *Ostrya virginiana* | hop hornbeam | Tree | No | No | | X | | |
| *Paulownia tomentosa* | princess tree | Tree | Yes | Yes | | X | | |
| *Prenanthes altissima* | rattlesnake root | Herb | No | No | | X | | |
| *Prunus virginiana* | choke cherry | Tree | No | No | | X | | |
| *Rubus hispidus* | swamp dewberry | Herb | No | No | | X | | |
| *Rubus occidentalis* | black raspberry | Herb | No | No | | X | | |
| *Rubus recurvicaulis* | dewberry | Herb | No | No | | X | | |
| *Lactuca canadensis* | wild lettuce | Herb | No | No | | X | | X |
| *Ulmus rubra* | slippery elm | Tree | No | No | | X | | X |
| *Geum virginianum* | cream-colored avens | Herb | No | No | | X | X | |
| *Quercus alba* | white oak | Tree | No | No | | X | X | |
| *Acer platanoides* | Norway maple | Tree | Yes | Yes | | X | X | X |
| *Arisaema triphyllum* | Jack-in-the-pulpit | Herb | No | No | | X | X | X |
| *Fraxinus americana* | white ash | Tree | No | No | | X | X | X |
| *Galium circaezans* | wild licorice | Herb | No | No | | X | X | X |
| *Podophyllum peltatum* | may-apple | Herb | No | No | | X | X | X |
| *Quercus rubra* | northern red oak | Tree | No | No | | X | X | X |
| *Rhodotypos scandens* | jetbead | Herb | Yes | No | | X | X | X |
| *Rosa multiflora* | multiflora rose | Shrub | Yes | Yes | | X | X | X |
| *Berberis thunbergii* | Japanese barberry | Shrub | Yes | No | X | | | |
| *Hackelia virginiana* | beggar's lice | Herb | No | No | X | | | |
| *Lobelia inflata* | Indian tobacco | Herb | No | No | X | | | |
| *Trillium* sp. | trillium | Herb | No | No | X | | | |
| *Viburnum dentatum* | arrowwood viburnum | Shrub | No | No | X | | | |
| *Symphyotrichum divaricatum* | white wood aster | Herb | No | No | X | | | X |
| *Cryptotaenia canadensis* | honewart | Herb | No | No | X | | X | |
| *Duchesnea indica* | Indian strawberry | Herb | Yes | No | X | | X | |
| *Galium triflorum* | sweet-scented bedstraw | Herb | No | No | X | | X | |

| Scientific name | Common name | Plant type | Exotic[a] | Invasive[b] | 1993 | 1995 | 1998 | 2003 |
|---|---|---|---|---|---|---|---|---|
| *Alliaria petiolata* | garlic-mustard | Herb | Yes | Yes | X | | X | X |
| *Cardamine impatiens* | bitter-cress | Herb | Yes | No | X | | X | X |
| *Liriodendron tulipifera* | tuliptree | Tree | No | No | X | | X | X |
| *Prunus avium* | sweet cherry | Tree | Yes | No | X | | X | X |
| *Fagus grandifolia* | American beech | Tree | No | No | X | X | | |
| *Malva neglecta* | common mallow | Herb | Yes | No | X | X | | |
| *Pastinaca sativa* | wild parsnip | Herb | Yes | No | X | X | | |
| *Phlox* sp. | phlox | Herb | No | No | X | X | | |
| *Vitis aestivalis* | summer grape | Vine | No | No | X | X | | |
| *Geranium carolinianum* | wild geranium | Herb | No | No | X | X | | X |
| *Oxalis stricta* | common yellow wood-sorrel | Herb | No | No | X | X | | X |
| *Polygonum caespitosum* | smartweed | Herb | Yes | No | X | X | | X |
| *Amphicarpa bracteata* | hog peanut | Herb | No | No | X | X | X | |
| *Athyrium filix-femina* | northern lady fern | Herb | No | No | X | X | X | |
| *Betula lenta* | black birch | Tree | No | No | X | X | X | |
| *Cercis canadensis* | redbud | Tree | No | No | X | X | X | |
| *Cornus florida* | flowering dogwood | Tree | No | No | X | X | X | |
| *Pilea pumila* | clearweed | Herb | No | No | X | X | X | |
| *Sanicula marilandica* | black snake root | Herb | No | No | X | X | X | |
| *Acer rubrum* | red maple | Tree | No | No | X | X | X | X |
| *Carex gracilescens* | sedge | Herb | No | No | X | X | X | X |
| *Carya* sp. | hickory | Tree | No | No | X | X | X | X |
| *Celastrus orbiculatus* | Oriental bittersweet | Vine | Yes | Yes | X | X | X | X |
| *Circaea alpina* | enchanter's nightshade | Herb | No | No | | X | X | X |
| *Hepatica nobilis* | liverleaf | Herb | No | No | | X | X | X |
| *Kalmia latifolia* | mountain laurel | Shrub | No | No | | X | X | X |
| *Ligustrum vulgare* | common privet | Shrub | Yes | Yes | | X | X | X |
| *Lindera benzoin* | spicebush | Shrub | No | No | | X | X | X |
| *Lonicera japonica* | Japanese honeysuckle | Vine | Yes | Yes | | X | X | X |
| *Maianthemum racemosum* | false Solomon's seal | Herb | No | No | | X | X | X |
| *Microstegium vimineum* | stilt grass | Herb | Yes | Yes | | X | X | X |
| *Nyssa sylvatica* | blackgum | Tree | No | No | | X | X | X |
| *Osmorhiza claytoni* | sweet cicely | Herb | No | No | | X | X | X |
| *Parthenocissus quinquefolia* | Virginia creeper | Vine | No | No | | X | X | X |
| *Polygonatum* sp. | Solomon's seal | Herb | No | No | | X | X | X |

| Scientific name | Common name | Plant type | Exotic[a] | Invasive[b] | 1993 | 1995 | 1998 | 2003 |
|---|---|---|---|---|---|---|---|---|
| *Polygonum virginianum* | jumpseed | Herb | No | No | X | X | X | X |
| *Quercus montana* | chestnut oak | Tree | No | No | X | X | X | X |
| *Rubus phoenicolasius* | wineberry | Herb | Yes | Yes | X | X | X | X |
| *Sanguinaria canadensis* | bloodroot | Herb | No | No | X | X | X | X |
| *Sassafras albidum* | sassafras | Tree | No | No | X | X | X | X |
| *Toxicodendron radicans* | poison ivy | Vine | No | No | X | X | X | X |
| *Uvularia perfoliata* | bellwort | Herb | No | No | X | X | X | X |
| *Vaccinium* sp. / *Gaylussacia* sp. | blueberry | Shrub | No | No | X | X | X | X |
| *Viburnum acerifolium* | maple-leaf viburnum | Shrub | No | No | X | X | X | X |
| *Viburnum prunifolium* | black haw | Shrub | No | No | X | X | X | X |
| *Viola* sp. | violet | Herb | No | No | X | X | X | X |

[a] Rhoads, A. F., and W. M. Klein, Jr. 1993. The Vascular Flora of Pennsylvania: Annotated Checklist and Atlas. American Philosophical Society. Philadelphia, PA.

[b] Invasive: Pennsuylvania Department of Conservation and Natural Resources. 2005. Invasive Exotic Plant Managment Tutorial for Natural Lands Managers. Mid-Atlantic Exotic Pest Plant Council, Inc. Lisa Smith, Principal Investigator. http://www.dcnr.state.pa.us/forestry/invasivetutorial/List.htm.

NPS D-107  April 2008

www.ingramcontent.com/pod-product-compliance
Lightning Source LLC
Chambersburg PA
CBHW080907290526
45795CB00007BA/2443